Teenage Nervous Breakdown

Music and Politics in the Post-Elvis Age

Previously published by David Walley

No Commercial Potential: The Saga of Frank Zappa

The Ernie Kovacs Phile

Teenage Nervous Breakdown

Music and Politics in the Post-Elvis Age

David Walley

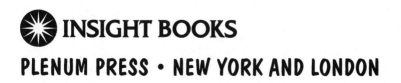

INSIGHT BOOKS

PLENUM PRESS • NEW YORK AND LONDON

Library of Congress Cataloging-in-Publication Data

On file

ISBN 0-306-45862-4

© 1998 David Walley
Insight Books is a Division of Plenum Publishing Corporation
233 Spring Street, New York, N.Y. 10013-1578

http://www.plenum.com

An Insight Book

Printed in the United States of America

To Jim Morrison, Duane Allman, and Vivian Stanshall,
but especially Lowell George

You will find yourself describing the birth pangs of a new culture, because the old one is dead and doesn't even know it.

—KURT VONNEGUT

Contents

Preface

Somewhere back in the midseventies I chanced upon an essay by Kurt Vonnegut called "Good Missiles, Good Manners, Good Night," wherein he relayed the comments of an Indianapolis luncheon companion with an "upper-class Hoosier" accent who said this:

> When you get to be our age, you all of a sudden realize that you were being ruled by the people you went to high school with. . . . You all of a sudden catch on that life is nothing *but* high school. You make a fool of yourself in high school, then you go in to college and learn how you should have acted in high school, and then you get out into real life, and that turns out to be high school all over again—class officers, cheerleaders, and all.[1]

Of course, he was right, but because it's been happening for a few generations now, most of us have all but ceased to notice it—we are resigned to it in fact. So was I until faced with the prospect of going through adolescence yet again, but through the eyes and feelings of my eldest daughter (11 but going on 16 as kids increasingly seem to be nowadays). This book is as much for my generation as for hers who will, in time, I suppose, wonder about the same thing.

We all know that being a teenager and having to endure high school sucks, and the sooner it's over the better. If this is true, I'm puzzled why we as a nation *willingly* continue to haunt the corridors of rock and roll high school, but now as hostages to a system (and state of mind) that encourages our adolescent

9

selves, needs, desires, fears, and tastes rather than getting on with our lives in the present tense. As a cultural historian, I've devoted most of my adult creative life to being fascinated and intrigued by how we got to this point in our national development. Who really made the dance steps it seems we all have to learn? Even our national political campaigns resemble high school student body politics, some not even as clever. What for newer New Age journalists is that "ultimate" litmus test of character? How the candidates were in high school, especially for elections in this Post-Elvis Age, post-1978.

Why the "Post-Elvis Age," you ask? It was during the career of Elvis Presley from 1954 to 1977 that America and by extension rock and roll music made its mark on the world: as an attitude as well a sonic environment for commerce. "This, Here, Soon" (Chapter 1) will explain when and how this happened by placing it within its historical context.

The essays and philippics in *Teenage Nervous Breakdown* are my attempt to examine the ramifications of this continuing state of affairs by focusing on the many interfaces between music and politics. It will examine how a state of mind that originated in fifties high school culture and peer group morals has been culturally and commercially exploited, and in what ways our lives and our world (including the nature of American democracy) have been altered in the process. While this secular teenage religion with its broad-based multinational and ideological appeal promises to keep us young (in mind and spirit if not in body), it is simultaneously exacting a terrible price. Though the songs of youth (present and past) inform our lives and promote a sense of shared time and history, I've wondered whether it is even real or a collectively homogenized compilation of electronic media nostalgia that has been developed, perfected, and refined over the past 40 years of increasingly wired-in life in this global society. I've been thinking, in short, about time, time and those waves—cultural historians among others are fond of doing that.

Teenage Nervous Breakdown is basically a series of word-jazz rock and roll improvisations and variations on the above themes. I'd like them to be thought of as a jumping-off place, a platform that will provoke further investigations and dialogues about the nature of the beat and rhythm of contemporary American life. Instead of musical notes arranged in various time signatures, I'm using ideas from historians, economists, social scientists, poets, and rock and rollers too. Each essay has its own individual form and rhythm, but don't be fooled by the "time": "White Punks on Dope" (Chapter 9) for instance, might appear to be an academic essay—it's not, trust me. Some essays have extensive endnotes and structure, others are little more than free form—that's where I'm riffing, taking a solo. "The Book of Head" in "Blame It on the Sixties" (Chapter 3), and most of "Don't Touch Me There" (Chapter 8) are examples of that I suppose.

Relax and enjoy the set.

11

DAVID G. WALLEY
York, ME
October 3, 1997

Acknowledgments

I'd like to thank the following people, without whom this book could not have been written:

These people provided inspiration in the past tense: Warren Susman, L. B. Namier, M. Gale Hoffman, and Jacques LeGrande.

These people provided insight and encouragement in the present tense: MacAlister "Mac" Brown; Russell Bostert of Williams College; the staff of Sawyer Library, Williams College, especially Walter Komorowski, a prince among archivists; the staff of Williamstown Public Library; Jim Reed and Bill Leach, savvy historians and good friends; Paul Barrère, who, fresh from the shower, provided me with the lyrics for "Teenage Nervous Breakdown" and Elizabeth George's address; and Michael Ochs for aid and comfort, just like old times.

A special tip of the head to Nigey Lennon for listening to huge chunks of this book over the phone, even if she didn't have a clue of the context and for stepping in as a pinch-hitting editor for "Boxers or Briefs"; to The Galactic Editrix who ran this whole manuscript through her magic fingers while mercilessly chastising me for being a comma murderer; to my rock and roll agent, Joe Regal, a.k.a Dr. Jazz, who took time he didn't have to fine tune "Blame It on the Sixties" even though he wasn't born then.

Geli, my only wife, and our four children, Sean, KC, Lindsay, and Melissa, I thank for putting up with me being abstracted and "out of it" in the course of this project. I'm sure they're glad to have me back for a while.

Last, I'd like to thank Don Gifford, my good friend, mentor, and the unindicted coconspirator who, over lunch 4 years ago, suggested I stop ranting long enough to actually sit down and write this book. Throughout this project, he has kept me on track and focused. His insights on American cultural history, the Transcendentalists, and Henry James and his crowd, as well as jazz history, have been invaluable. I especially thank him for bringing to my attention Louis Jordan and the Timpani Five. I feel truly blessed to have been able to collaborate with such a scholar. It's been one hell of a ride, hasn't it, Don?

Chapter 1
This, Here, Soon"[1]

Growing Up

it's like the high dive
    at camp
you went up one way
and you came down another
you could either dive or jump
but you couldn't go back
    down the ladder.
some kids stood there
all thru lunch
but the counsellor
wouldn't let them climb
    down
and the longer you waited
the harder it got.

I did one of those life saving jumps
the kind with my arms and legs spread
but I still splat the water pretty hard
    it stung.

PEGGY GARRISON[2]

The younger generation begins in the womb; before it is three years old, major industries . . . are vying for its favor. By the time it is in its teens, its purchasing power is immense; and it has by then developed a social style of its own, which older generations react to, chiefly with aversion but to some extent with emulation.

GILBERT OSTRANDER[3]

In the Post-Elvis Age our collective perception of our history as a people and the cultural time of our nation have been fundamentally altered. Both have been held hostage by the corrosive effects of an increasingly celebrity-driven consumerism, itself the result of the cumulative effects of the commercial exploitation of high school peer group dynamics that started in the fifties, whose present market share has, as of this writing, been computed to be a whopping $65 billion per annum. During and after the Age of Elvis, this virulent form of goods-driven, not to mention intellectual, consumerism animated by the rock and roll beat has in turn affected our world to the point where a multinational corporate consciousness has replaced our sense of selves. In a little more than a quarter century, these marketing techniques now sell all manner of goods and services, its reach further extended by music television, which broadcasts its visual equivalent 24 hours a day, 7 days a week—our new Voice of America.

In those epochal years from 1954 to 1977 in which Elvis Presley's and the Beatles' careers bloomed and sputtered, rock and roll had succeeded in transforming our collective character. By the early sixties, adolescence, an uncomfortable waystation on the way to maturity—formerly a matter of age or attitude—had become not only a big business, an infinitely renewable commercial resource, but also a desirable state of being all by itself. At one time it may have been that all you needed was love, but now a credit card or two is more than helpful to pay for the rock and roll dreams that money can buy. Today the economic power of youth has become the principal fuel that powers the great multinational entertainment conglomerates to an extent that even a decade ago was impossible to conceive. This state of affairs didn't happen overnight. These tendencies have been inherent in America's character from its inception—we've just ignored them.

In 1835 when Alexis de Tocqueville, a French aristocrat, wrote *Democracy in America*, he was fascinated by the vitality of a young America and its drive to be a great independent commercial power, although he had some reservations about that goods-oriented *now*. He did not question America's being, its commercial spirit, but he was struck by what it could become as a result:

> . . . not that it leads men away from the pursuit of forbidden enjoyments, but that it absorbs them wholly in quest of those which are allowed. By these means, a kind of virtuous materialism may ultimately be established in the world which would not corrupt, but enervate, the soul, and noiselessly unbend the springs of action.[4]

Two decades later while roaming the streets of Brooklyn and Jersey City, Walt Whitman, enamored, enraptured, and lyrically drunk on the fumes of American possibilities, wrote *Democratic Vistas*. Like de Tocqueville, he was aware of his nation's *now*, but still held a consciousness of *then*, of America's immediate past in the age of steam and rails, as well as of its immediate future in the Civil War and the era of the robber barons to come. He faced toward the future that he saw from the vantage point of his epochal poetic *now:*

> America, betaking herself to formative action (as it is about time for more solid achievement, and less windy promise.), must, for her purposes, cease to recognize a theory of character grown of feudal aristocracies, or form'd by merely literary standards, or from any ultramarine, full-dress formulas of culture, polish, caste, &c., enough, and must sternly promulgate her new standard, yet old enough, and accepting the old, the perennial elements, and combining them into groups, unities, appropriate to

the modern, the democratic, the west, and to the practical occasions and needs of our own cities, and of the agricultural regions.[5]

Quite obviously, Whitman's Democratic Vistas, his speculations, never envisioned multinational conglomerates built upon the commercial possibilities of adolescent consumers becoming bigger ones with more expensive tastes. Or the economies built upon educating preteen and preschool consumers how to step logically from Power Ranger/Ninja Turtle battle axes to Air Jordans to BMWs in their own consumer-affinity groupings. Who knows what he would have made of the debate that has raged for a quarter century about the cumulative effect on children of sex and violence on TV or in movies? How would he have assessed the advertisers who sponsor and package such shows or the commercials themselves? Or the corrosive effects of commercials on the national mind and on the youth who spend a total of 2 months of waking hours per year alone watching them?[6] Yes, these are modern problems for the modern age that Whitman couldn't have foreseen. Nevertheless, it is remarkable that, despite this apparent weakness of vision to our the modern sensibility, he intuited the path America had taken as well as the crisis it would provoke down the road:

19

> I say of this tremendous and dominant play of solely materialistic bearings upon current life in the United States, with the result as already seen, accumulating, and reaching far into the future, that they must either be confronted and met by at least an equally subtle and tremendous force-infusion of purposes of spiritualization, for the pure conscience, for genuine aesthetics, and for absolute and primal manliness and womanliness—otherwise our modern civilization, with all its improvements, is in vain, and we are on the road to a destiny, a status, equivalent, in this real world, to that of the fabled damned.[7]

Fate of the "fabled damned"? That's one hell of a punishment for straying from the idealistic ethical path he envisioned America should and could follow. But without a map-building childhood or an adolescence free from external commercial

manipulation, what other course is available? What you see is
what you get now, because America's greatest industry, its
major export to the world, is devoted to making products mediated on the *now*-ness of a promised collective mythical future
that aims to negate the *then* of the past forever, just as our rock
and roll world does.

In the roaring twenties, 60 years after Whitman's *Vistas*,
Johan Huizinga, the renowned Dutch medievalist historian, arrived on these shores to an America booming in the aftermath
of World War I, a war that had plunged everyone into a bloody,
pointless, and destructive frame of *now*—in the words of Ezra
Pound "For an old bitch gone in the teeth,/For a botched civilization."[8] Like Whitman and de Tocqueville before him,
Huizinga was also impressed by the force of America's militant
present-tense living. In a series of collected lectures and observations entitled *America: A Dutch Historian's Vision, From Afar
and Near*, he summarized the American experience of "This,
Here, Soon" as indicative of its enthusiastic acceptance of life in
the present and future tense.

And like de Tocqueville and Whitman, he saw that despite
its commercial and social energy there was also another force
working on the spirit of America:

> . . . a perpetual tension in America between a passionate ide-
> alism and an unrestrainable energy directed to material things.
> And because the popular mind in America is naive and easily
> moved emotionally, it often does not observe the contradiction
> between what the country does and its resounding democratic
> ideals.[9]

Although the Great Depression of the thirties may have
briefly administered a shock to America's consumer appetite,
the shock did not last; the industrial boom generated by World
War II and its aftermath rocketed America into an unparalleled
material prosperity. For some at the dawn of the modern consumer era in the late forties, notably clergymen and scholars

like Joseph Harountunian, there was a profound and disquieting moral crisis afoot amidst this explosive, unnatural, and surreal abundance that

> . . . tempts men to be at once fascinated and repelled by the good. It tempts men to pursue goods, and in doing so, to fear the good. The good is in "justice, mercy and peace". It is consistency and integrity, in loving according to truth and right. It inheres in men and not in things. It is other than the goodness of goods and without it, goods are not good. But the machine-made spirit teaches otherwise. It identifies the good with goods and induces men to dread it except as thus identified. It persuades men that there is no good other than goods. Thus men come to dread good as evil and to love evil as good. Thus it is that an apparent good produces evil.[10]

Harountunian's dire remarks may have well suited certain segments of the population to whom consumer culture was still a novelty (and some today), but nearly a half century later, after the Pill, credit cards, microchips, and the Internet, his lofty homiletics seem quaint and arcane to the majority of Americans. For them, the Depression and World War II are as so much black-and-white film footage. And although the machine-made world in which we easily abide is deemed user-friendly, more than ever America's watchwords remain "This, Here, Soon."

Morality in a consumer society? Get real: Goods are goods, they're morally neutral, some are better or worse, and about the only time the question comes up is just about the time you've paid for your car or the warranty has expired and it dies (how do they do that?). Only then do you find out that these days "durable goods" are by definition only supposed to last 3 years. If anything, moral rights have become consumer rights—all we need are tighter lemon laws since everyone's a consumer, no? That's the way we've all been schooled, and that goes to the heart of the matter, as we'll find out.

And despite the fact that our playroom remains continually stocked with an inexhaustible surfeit of goods, there is an undercurrent of discontent, a notion of consequences that comes from the selective art of consumer forget. What do we do when we tire of our goods, our toys? According to Bill Bryson, former expatriate American journalist living in England, we banish them and the *then* they represent to the perennial garage, attic, or hall closet

> . . . [which] seem to be always full of yesterday's enthusiasms: golf clubs, scuba diving equipment, tennis rackets, exercise machines, tape recorders, darkroom equipment, objects that once excited their owner and then were replaced by other objects even more shiny and exciting. That is the great seductive thing about America—the people always get what they want, right now, whether it is good for them or not. There is something deeply worrying, and awesomely irresponsible, about this endless self-gratification, this constant appeal to the baser instincts.[11]

Though the *nows* of de Tocqueville and Bryson are separated by more than 150 years, their observations neatly dovetail into each other. The problem they uncover deep within the collective American psyche has come to a critical juncture, this result of living without the presence of a past. In Whitman's time it was common to complain that, compared to Europe, America had no past and no culture of its own. It did; it just wasn't on the order of Sir Walter Scott's *Ivanhoe*—it was different, uniquely American, and Longfellow wrote *Hiawatha* in the attempt to fill that void, as did James Fenimore Cooper with the *Deerslayer*. In this Post-Elvis Age, TV, computers, and rock and roll music are supposed to be equivalents, but what do they say?

Back in the fifties, at the dawn of the modern era of TV, Ernie Kovacs, one of the pioneers in electronically enhanced TV comedy, was quoted as saying, "Don't watch too much TV, it will only rot your mind."[12] He may have been right, but that's not all it's done. While today Ernie Kovacs is hailed for the creation and development of a unique comedic electronic visual vocabulary, he was looked on in his time as a loveable if quirky eccentric. An exception in the so-called Golden Age of Television, he managed to succeed despite, not because of, the possibilities already inherent in the intoxicating mixture of commerce and entertainment. TV exerted its fascination not only on adult Americans of the post-War generation who were comparatively new to it, but also on a bumper crop of children. For preschoolers in the fifties, it was an electronic babysitter to give Mom a break, and when the older school-age children trooped in after school it served as company so that the evening meal could be prepared and on the table at 5:30 when Dad came home. Such diversions included not only *Romper Room* or *Kukla Fran and Ollie* in the morning but also afterschool teen dance shows like Dick Clark's *American Bandstand* (and its regional equivalents), which publicized the music of Elvis Presley, Jerry Lee Lewis, and others. Wildly successful of course were Walt Disney's *Mickey Mouse Club* and *The Wonderful World of Disney*, which in 1955 launched not only a theme-park way of life and national merchandizing fads but also a media conglomerate lifestyle/ideology of considerable economic and cultural strength that still exists today. During this "Golden Age" an enduring connection was cemented between Mickey Mouse and rock and roll (more on that later), through which merchandizing techniques were developed and refined that would appeal to teenagers and future generations of teenagers as well.

According to Steven Kline, a Canadian media researcher, in his book *Out of the Garden: Toys and Children's Culture in the Age of TV Marketing*, it was in the service of the economic goals of Ronald Reagan's America that in the early eighties the children's TV industry was deregulated so that toy manufacturers were given free rein to produce half-hour cartoon infomercials to sell preschoolers and preteens their character toys. Ever the economic realist, Reagan was just levelling the playing field by expanding the reach of merchandizing practices already in place in the early fifties that had been dealing with young teen baby boomers and their uncommitted money, which now could ensnare preteens and toddlers in a market that was formerly off limits. Preteens are no longer considered passive; their "lifestyle preferences" are not only actively solicited and

tracked, but it's also commonplace these days for kids themselves to be consultants and junior art directors for toy companies.

Enough time has passed since the fifties, so there's a
closed feedback loop operating under these unifying premises:
Habituate children early to the values of the broker's world even
though they might not immediately have the direct purchasing
power, for eventually when they become teens they'll demand
their own goods just like their sisters, brothers, and parents before them. Finally it was possible for younger and younger children to be exploited by larger and larger industries for, as it
turns out, bigger and bigger bucks. In the nineties, this seems to
be an acceptable situation despite the consequences it has on all
of us of whatever age. It's an ironic comment on American life
that if you want to find out about children in this shopper's paradise, you ask the marketers and brokers rather than child or
adolescent psychologists; anyway, grown-ups are now just bigger
kids, aren't they? Still, there's nothing sadder in a growing
child's room than last year's hottest toy lying forlorn and abandoned and stuffed into a corner (and if ideas were toys, what
then?).

Now-America guarantees that ghosts of goods past never
interfere with the promise of today's playroom, since they can
be unloaded on the world after-market—everything from pesti-
cides to TV reruns of *Seinfeld* (or cluster bombs, land mines, or
even jet fighters), there's limitless room for expansion. In *Now*-
America there is no time for reflection; the system we've put in
place discourages introspection. As we approach the twenty-first
century, we hold on not only to our toys but also to the preado-
lescent attitudes that go with them. In doing so, the brokers of
the present without the presence of a past have succeeded in
short-circuiting our natural development—effectively changing
our national motto from *E Pluribus Unum* to *Whoever Dies
with the Most Toys, Wins* in the process so we'll never be
without our toys.

How has it happened that although America is a world power we haven't yet managed to graduate from high school? The consumerist addiction that has brought us to this pinnacle of power, which animated our becoming, now inhibits our growth and threatens our survival. This consumerist addiction prevents us from seeing who and what we are by substituting a continuous stream of images of what we should be that arrests our social, cultural, and intellectual development—the signs are everywhere. We are first exposed to this system in high school, to the idea that we have vested rights in consumer society. It is here where we are first encouraged to "keep up" with no critical thought about what we are "keeping up." And to be forever in high school holds us focused on today with no consciousness of yesterday, so there will never be any continuity with tomorrow, with fatal political and cultural consequences.

In America today, there is no *then*, only *now:* that's how we Americans defeat and neutralize time, the creator/destroyer. Without a presence of a past, there never will be need for any other time, either. There is no room for history because that was *then*, that's old, and as a nation we think of ourselves forever young, right? "That was then but this is now" is also the mantra for the current generation of twenty-somethings, the first real generation of the Post-Elvis Age who've been brought up in the postmodern, or rather postcultural, age of TV, electronic mail, and MTV buzz clips.

The *now* of this first full generation to truly surf the Virtual Reality Channel has convinced them (and the rest of us) that everything can be mixed, matched, controlled, and downloaded with the click of a mouse, and so by extension, the world off-screen can be altered. The creators of *Now*-America have convinced this generation of the possibility that anything is possible, as long as they cede control of their being and becoming and allow themselves to be completely disconnected from their individual *nows*. Speaking to (and for) them in specialized, demographically correct, and comforting tones that surround the

images of the rock and roll world, the promoters and brokers of
Now-America humbly and dispassionately perform their services. *Now*-America comforts this ever-renewable market safely
inside its self-referential cultural bubble. If it seems there's no
longer any reference points, no matter, the kids are already
used to it now. As long as the vision looks cool and appears exclusive and readily available from somewhere or someone—
preferably downloaded so you don't have to leave home—that's
enough.

Unfortunately here's a high price paid for having no *then*
in the electronic *now*, for being comfortable within this consumer world of competing brokers. In exchange for this endless
parade of goods, services, and lifestyle possibilities, the creators
of the *now* have expropriated each generation's singular child-
hoods and imaginations and successfully converted them into
shares of the nostalgia futures market in a blink of the eye.

If *Now*-America had a living concept of its history that
wasn't largely defined and characterized by a nostalgia for
goods past, perhaps there wouldn't be the confusion and conflict that alienate and fester in the souls of the young and are
rapidly becoming *the* issues in our national life as our present
affects our future. If America and Americans came to terms
with the past in the present, she (and we) wouldn't be so continually astonished and appalled by this crisis, which in one form
or other has been with us for 150 years.

According to our leading intellectuals, the reason all of us
"normal" citizens are frazzled, spooked, and in crisis is that
we're having trouble dealing with life in the postmodernist
world. Best forget the "crisis of postmodernism" hurting our
heads for a moment and check out those rock and roll shoes
pinching our feet, if not wearing them out altogether. Our crisis
is really the result of living in the Post-Elvis Age, a sociocultural
philosophical state far more precarious than the "end of history" that official intellectuals like Francis Fukayama preach

when they blame everything culturally entropic on the fall of the Soviet Union. To him, that formerly dark political Other was the prime engine of cultural change whose recent collapse and eclipse has put all the politicians, foundation groupies, and think tank intellectuals like himself out of a job and left the rest of us twitching. And because we've lost Mother Russia as the schoolyard bully figure to oppose, that's why we're dozing and drooling, as if we've been blinded by the light—maybe Fukayama's boys are, but not the rest of us. They could just as easily have turned on the pop media to find something closer to home whose effects are more pandemic. Whether he and they want to acknowledge it or not, many of his under-60 colleagues who were born into, during, and soon-to-be-after Age of Elvis get as much, or perhaps more, of their intellectual sustenance and world view from the word, music, and philosophy of the Grateful Dead (or Nirvana, Oasis, Madonna, or any one-hit wonder group on the charts) as they do from contemplating the geopolitical strategies of Bismarck, Prince Metternich, Tallyrand, Seulieman the Magnificent, or Henry Kissinger, for that matter.

27

For many cultural conservatives, especially Allan Bloom and William Bennett, rock and roll is the bête noir, the great beast that is the cause of the end of history as they know it. For Bloom, rock and roll stirs children's sexuality toward a Dionysian frenzy:

> It acknowledges the first emanations of children's emerging sensuality and addresses them seriously, eliciting them and legitimating them, not as little sprouts that must be carefully tended in order to grow into gorgeous flowers, but as the real thing. Rock given children on a silver platter, with all the public authority of the entertainment industry, is everything their parents used to tell them they had to wait until they grew up and would understand later.[13]

So nu? This is not a great revelation; everyone knows in America that sex sells everything, not just music. Nor does anyone have to wait very long in this consumer world for the "next thing" to make us cool and with it to please our adolescent selves. Likewise, his description of the rock and roll child as a monster could easily apply to American society in general,

> . . . whose body throbs with orgasmic rhythms; whose feelings are made articulate in hymns to joy of onanism or the killing of parents; whose ambition is to win fame and wealth in imitating the drag-queen who makes the music. In short, life is made into a nonstop, commercially prepackaged masturbatory fantasy.[14]

What Bloom and his intellectual fellow-travelers should have understood is that rock is an *effect* of high school consumerism, not the *cause* of what ails America. The engine of adolescent consumerism makes the beat go on.

While rock and roll developed during the Age of Elvis into a gigantic economic force in its own right, the worlds of Kissinger, Seulieman, Mozart, Aristotle, et al. existed (and had existed) in simultaneously interlocking universes. Although separate, these worlds coexisted more or less in balance if not always in harmony. Since the midseventies and now in the Post-Elvis Age, however, this weave and texture, this complex interlocking cultural universe, has been gradually altered, and that sense of balance has been compromised. And this has less to do with the decline of the Soviet Union and more to do with rock and roll music politics than most official cultural historians and political theorists would like to admit.

In today's rock and roll world, the boundaries between music, politics, and consumerism are indistinct; after a while it hardly registers, save in egregious examples, like most recently the use of the Chambers Brothers' sixties anthem "Time (Has Come Today)," which back then was a call for political and intellectual liberation but now touts life insurance and financial planning to the very group that eschewed such concerns. Truly, the commercial is a consummate exercise in irony that uses that musical emotional hook to nail all those aging baby boomers who now are seriously thinking about a mortality that little concerned them in their paisley-colored youth. Of course, to everyone else not so emotionally involved and a few generations removed, it's just a catchy jingle. Still, it's a potent piece of commerce.

Just how permeable the cultural membrane is between the worlds of rock music and politics was demonstrated in 1995 when Jerry Garcia, the lead guitarist of the Grateful Dead, an iconic sixties countercultural institution, passed on. The flood of tributes emanating not only from the usual suspects, pop commentators and the like, but also from the floor of the Senate and the House of Representatives and even higher levels of government was extraordinary.

It was a little short of astonishing to see the Very Venerable Senator Patrick Leahy from Vermont appearing on the TV show *Nightline* the evening of Garcia's death not only to talk about his love for the Dead's music but also to present an informed appreciation of the lifestyle and attitude the Dead's music promoted to kids of all ages. No less astounding was the decision of the Yale-educated governor of Massachusetts, William Weld, the last person one would suspect of being a closet Deadhead, to order all state flags lowered to half-mast in tribute to Jerry's long strange trip (and it *wasn't* even an election year!). Garcia's obituary also appeared in different forms throughout the world, such was the band's impact on the world.

29

The Age of Elvis had already left a sizeable footprint on American diplomacy when in 1990 Vaclav Havel, president of the Czech Republic and one of the cofounders of the Republic's Velvet Revolution (and a far more committed intellectual than Francis Fukayama) met Frank Zappa, a man whose music and ideas had inspired Czech students in Prague to battle Soviet tanks with rocks in the late sixties. It was said that Soviet secret policemen at the time of the uprising, while beating students during their "interrogations," used to mutter under their breath that they were going to "beat the Zappa" out of them.[15] To some of Havel's generation who survived to become masters of their own political destiny 20 years down the road. Zappa and his music were a vital part of their living contemporary cultural and political history. To acknowledge those contributions, on behalf of the Czech people, Havel decided to appoint Frank as the Czech Republic's representative on matters of trade, culture, and tourism to promote their economic interests abroad. As a gesture to the rock and roll world in which Havel's contemporaries lived, it was fitting and proper, but as they say, no good deed goes unpunished.

Upon hearing about this appointment from the American diplomats in Prague (as well as Zappa's on-the-record comment to Havel that spending even 5 minutes with American vice president Dan Quayle was a colossal waste of time), James Baker, Secretary of State, stepped into the breach to defend America's honor. Dramatically and unexpectedly, Baker made an eleventh-hour stop in Prague on his way to a Bush/Gorbachev summit to notify Havel and his baffled ministers that such an appointment would be considered a grave affront to the United States; if the appointment wasn't rescinded there would be "consequences."[16]

What Havel did not know was that for the Bush Administration (and the Reagan Administration before it), Zappa had consistently been a trouble-maker, a major ideological irritant who not only had the unmitigated audacity to mercilessly criticize and satirize Reagan's involvement with and dependence on the support of the Religious Right, but had also made Baker's wife and other highly connected political spouses targets of ridicule because of their stance on music censorship (more on this elsewhere). Havel in his sublime hippie innocence (and view of cultural politics) had stumbled into a major diplomatic gaffe, the last thing he needed if he wanted to beg economic boons from his Uncle Sam.

What actually transpired behind closed doors has so far not been revealed, but Havel backed down. Zappa's credentials were revoked, and business, one supposes, has gone on as usual ever since. In retrospect, the whole incident was laughable, diplomatic niceties and idiot national pride aside; everyone knew what the story was and who the laugh was really on. Still, the politics of entertainment and the politics of international diplomacy were as close as they'd ever been before or since, too. Only in America in the Post-Elvis Age would this have been possible.

Judging from the reams of tributes that flowed from the world's press when the King passed to his final reward on August 16, 1977, rock and roll had attained its majority. Elvis had achieved world citizenship right up there with Gandhi, JFK, and the Pope (whichever one had died), and his passing put a power spike into our collective electronic soul. Although in death Elvis may have become a nostalgia piece who died a drug-addled Las Vegas lounge lizard or, for some, a parody of himself whose own music had little relevance to the world lifestyle he had midwifed, the world he presided over even in exile had become a protean force by itself. Certainly rock and roll has never forgotten the King, for subsequently he has become a focus of a pop mystery cult. Graceland, his Memphis home, is now a shrine-like Lourdes for the faithful—while his life and death have been the subject of numerous popular sensationalist and scholarly academic works and conferences and TV movies. So the rock and roll world continues to expand into every aspect of our lives.

31

It's a depressing truism that the music of youth (past and present) seems more and more to be a product conceived to appeal as much to the corporate bottom line as it is to the audience whose aural background the music inhabits, to the detriment of both creators and listeners. And we've allowed this to happen, too, have given up the struggle. These days, up-and-coming bands who think that art is stronger than cash are rudely awakened when they learn it costs anywhere from $500 to $1000 per song to break into local, regional, or national charts, according to anonymous industry sources. Cash or digital equipment does the trick for many program directors—hey, that's the business. To hell with love, all you need is cash for that teenage American dream. And we ourselves can never get away from that consumer-nuanced peer group demographic we created in high school; it haunts us, so deeply we no longer know how to get out of the loop.

Chapter **2**

Who Stole the Bomp
(from the Bomp Sha Bomp)?

One of the most important aspects of post punk dissolution of rock certainties was the replacement of authenticity by artifice as the central concern in critical discourse.

SIMON FRITH[1]

Huh?

There's no denying it: Rock and roll criticism has come a long way since the fifties, when the only critical question that mattered was "can you dance to it?" (or make out, you know, "do the do," whatever that happened to be for you when you were young and fresh and fragrant). Forty years down the road in the nineties, dancing has taken a back seat to political content, correctness, and fashion death now that rock criticism has become an arena for respectable high-octane academic politics. Unfortunately, many of these master's essays and Ph.D. dissertations on punk rock and heavy metal—as well as other subcultural divisions—do not focus on the dynamic multicultural universe from whence they all came, but rather huckster the narrow-casted commercial vision that supplanted it. This new academic perspective, according to Ed Ward, a consistently clear-headed writer on music, has taken us all to a place where

> . . . the mystery has been completely taken away from rock and roll, that it has been over-explained, over-analyzed, and, in the process, it has become effectively neutered, incapable of shock and joy. . . . that for many "rock artists," the impulse toward fun has been smothered by an increasingly rigidified sense of what is and what isn't acceptable, destroyed by a flock of vultures who won't be sated until the corpse is picked clean, the roll removed from the rock, and every secret, no matter how trivial or irrelevant to the creative act, is laid bare.[2]

How this transformation from a simple background accompaniment of adolescence to a cultural foreground/obsession evolved and when it happened says as much about how the music's emotional meanings have been mutated by the commercial environment as the culture into which it has become its predominant soundtrack. Simply put: In the Post-Elvis Age, rock and roll has effectively changed this country's battle cry of "Give me liberty or give me death" to "Sex, drugs, and rock and roll." Or maybe it could be that the two have become covalent—"Give me liberty, sex, drugs, rock and roll, and death!" (probably in that order)—an even odder state of affairs.

Perhaps the new generation on the (cultural) block and the policeman's chorus of knee-jerk millenarians shrieking in the background are right. Everything appears to be going to hell in a handbasket anyway and the fat lady's obviously going to sing soon, so why bother: Let's party, to hell with it all. Then again, decadence has always been in fashion when a culture can't think of any coherent response to change. Even if this may appear to be so for some, it's instructive to see how we got here and how the larger priorities and values of music and its enjoyment have been over time transformed, if not completely compromised, in the process. The best perspective from which to view this crucial change is from that of the music press/media, which promoted and championed rock and roll, which spoke to and sometimes for its audience before it became a prize for multinational multimedia conglomerates to control if not devour whole. But let's rewind.

Back in the late fifties and into the early sixties, everyone knew rock and roll was about fucking, pure and simple; nobody came right out and said that openly, of course, you just had to read between the lines. Although the official safe Vaseline-smeared vision archtypically disseminated in George Lucas's film *American Graffiti*, said it was all about boys, girls, and parties (it's my party and I'll cry if I want to), it also promoted adolescent angst and alienation. For the rock and roll revivalists, it was primarily about cutting loose with your friends after school or riding up and down the main drag or around and around the town monument in your patched-together jalopy while scouting for the local hot action. (It's not like anyone really knew what to do with it if and when any was found, and weren't the mysteries of adolescent sex far more anecdotal in nature then than they are now?) There were girl groups and doo-wop groups, southern rhythm and blues, plus Elvis and "The Killer," Jerry Lee Lewis, Little Richard, and Fats Domino on Top 40 radio, and the great earth-shaking questions the songs posed were basically on the order of why fools fell in love with the leaders of the pack. Why indeed?

More to the point, rock and roll was part of the background of the fifties American life, a specialized soundtrack for the insular teen subculture of the sock hop and the prom as well as mood music for furtive rec room gropings, or summertime fun, harmless fun. This music for cruising came sluicing out of the Brill Building in New York, the songpluggers heaven, to answer these questions, to stroke teenage libidos, a strictly commercial product from music central just like it always had been since the radio daze of the thirties and forties for older generations. It had no secret meanings, no sociological insights, few cultural subtexts.

Time and those waves kicked in just as machine-made pop music was getting rather boring, formulaic, and safe, and along came the urban folk revival of the early sixties. It was music that filled the maturer needs of a still primarily literate generation of baby boom children who'd just graduated from cruising for burgers in Daddy's new car and were now going off to college, kids whose tastes were developing. Folk music provided an alternative to the Brill Building world, which churned out hit after hit, and the replicant teenage culture of Dick Clark's *American Bandstand* by offering its listeners a less packaged, more authentic American musical experience embodied in the rich folk music traditions of the Appalachians and in the blues from the south side of Chicago and the Mississippi Delta (another way back to rhythm and blues, true). It disseminated visions of not happy commerciality and sociological homogeneity of the post-

War fifties but of the cultural values and attitudes of that other America, of disenfranchised minorities, real people with real lives, windows into the true multicultural nature of America. The music also drew from folk forms and traditions not specifically American that stood apart from the official buttoned-down consumerist fifties culture. Magazines like *Sing Out!* sprang up for this audience, publishing song lyrics and music charts for pickers and singers while providing a forum for these artists themselves in which they could air their views, concerns, hopes, and desires.

When the raw blues energy of The Paul Butterfield Blues Band and the electric Bob Dylan merged with the energy of the Beatles and Rolling Stones, rhythm and blues became mixed and matched with the word; machine-made music was supplanted for a time by singer/songwriters and bands for whom all the news was fit to sing. For a moment, it seemed that there was a possibility of creating a multicultural world understanding built around music.* (The Beatles' experiments with Indian music spawned a whole raft of imitators and musical side trips as well as an interest in Middle Eastern and African music, which has come back around in the world music scene of today.) For the most part, though, this composite conglomerate music depended on words *and* music reflecting the musical tastes of a college generation that knew its Dostoyevsky, Brecht, Whitman, Vonnegut, and Ginsberg, but were equally at home with the music of Bach and Stravinsky; the boogie-woogie weaves of Professor Longhair, Eubie Blake, and John Lee Hooker; the blues stylings of Bessie Smith and Billie Holiday; and the jazz of Miles Davis, Charlie Parker, and John Coltrane.

For this reason, Bob Dylan's seminal electric albums, *Highway 61 Revisited, Bringing It All Back Home,* and *Blonde on Blonde* still continue to offer nourishment because their lit-

---

*Carlos Santana, lead guitarist of the legendary late-sixties band Santana, is rumored to have said that this happened sometime in the spring of 1970 for about 10 days to 2 weeks. It may have been longer, but not by much.

erary images were drawn from a much broader and richer cultural palate than from the involuted self-referential pop world. He wasn't speaking *at* his audience as much as *with* them; his morphing of rock and roll with blues/folk effectively inspired other artists and musicians to speak not only to each other in song but also to their audience in a common language: electric music for the body *and* mind.

In the early sixties, while television was packaging the "Swinging London"/Carnaby Street/visual-style *zeitgeist* of the British Invasion with TV shows like *Shindig* and *Hullabaloo*, the Brill Building mentality churned out one-shot fanzines devoted to particular mega-hit groups like the Beatles, Rolling Stones, and Monkees and similar packages for lesser-known groups. For the growing preteen market, which wanted to know what was out there to like, there were *Cheetah*, *Tiger Beat*, and *Hit Parader* magazines, which were highly cost-effective and easy to churn out. Essentially creations of mainstream magazine and newspaper publishers, these small in-house operations were composed of an editor, an advertising person, and a few editorial assistants from whom little more was required than their ability to reedit and rewrite canned public relations handouts (press releases, interviews, etc.) into preteen jargon while adequately art directing the fashion spreads, then ship.

Countering these chunks of processed printed cheese was the underground press, which appealed to the politically involved, or at least interested, college folk/blues enthusiasts; papers like the *San Francisco Oracle*, *East Village Other*, *Ann Arbor Argus*, and *Chicago Seed* covered radical politics and the anti-War and civil rights movements in all their hues. Textured into more challenging and innovative graphics were also articles on alternative lifestyles (well, not so "alternative" if one was a student of American social history of the Transcendentalists or radical French socialism of the nineteenth century). No paper worth its salt was complete without the freelance book and record reviewers and essayists who spoke to these issues.

From the underground press came music magazines specifically attuned to this same audience that focused on cultural politics. *Down Beat* in the fifties and *Jazz Magazine* in the early sixties (which by the late sixties became *Jazz and Pop*) were for the most part more cerebral, less political in their approach to music criticism. *Crawdaddy, Fusion, Changes, Rock,* and *Rolling Stone* (in its infancy) were magazines in which the official canons of rock criticism originated, the opinions and attitudes of which have become institutionalized in academia today. In its golden age from 1967 to 1972, music criticism produced writers like Greil Marcus, Langdon Winner, Robert Christgau, Robert Palmer, Ed Ward, Jim Miller, David Dalton, Ellen Willis, Robert Soma, Paul Nelson, and Paul Williams. Paul Williams, the founder of *Crawdaddy,* was the quintessential stylist for this new criticism, which mixed personal insights with freely associated literary and musical allusions.

In this time and place, for these writers and others like them, rock and roll was not only a window into modern life, but also a place where all kinds of cultural referents were at play, and not all specifically American in nature. Readers were accustomed to and expected a critical style that broadened the periphery of their ignorance. Thus it wasn't surprising in the middle of a discussion of an obscure country music ballad by Warren Smith called "Black Jack David," for instance, to come across a sidebar disquisition about the myth of Orpheus, Celtic mythology, Scottish ballads of the thirteenth century, or the English ballad tradition in the seventeenth century and its embryonic journey into the country music scene of 1966, exactly what Nick Toches did in *Country: The Twisted Roots of Rock 'n' Roll.*[5] No one even breathed hard, since the underlying assumption was that music culture did not exist in a vacuum but was part of a continuum of covalent cultural traditions.

One reason why this was so was that during the era of the Vietnam War and the draft, there was an abundance (a glut?) of grad students in humanities looking for creative outlets. What use was a liberal arts education, they asked themselves, if not to provide tools to understand the society and cultural environment in which they were participating? It's no surprise that many of these first-generation critics were either junior professors looking for a critical outlet or well-read and turned-on master of arts candidates in philosophy, sociology, history, and English doing the draft-dodger rag. It also followed that since most critics and musicians came from the same general educational background, they were also conversant with the same writers, painters, musicians, and philosophies, just like the audiences; music journalism was of a uniformly higher level.

The mind/body split that contaminated the New Left in the late sixties opened up a critical rift between those who viewed the music and its world in a broader interconnected cultural context and a new group of writers who appeared in the pages of Detroit's *Creem* magazine (the late Lester Bangs and Dave Marsh, among others). They viewed music (and virtually everything else) solely from the point of view of Midwestern teen America. The rock and roll world was the created flesh for these latter-day evangelists, these protectors of the Holy Grail of the New Rock Order, and their sworn duty was to keep it free from "foreign" contagion. No analysts need apply, no analysis necessary, thank you. To them and the constituency they represented, rock and roll spoke to *only* American kids in American high schools, working-class kids living working-class lives in the industrial heartland. It wasn't supposed to do anything to your mind except blow it; the only requirement was that it must be fun and could you party-vous? If you did, how stoned did you get? Was it survivable? And would you do it again?

All other approaches were effete, and the "art rock" those overeducated swells wrote about was for sissies, nerds, and dweebs, not red-blooded *American* teenagers. A dependable product that had a dependable effect, rock and roll was a virtual shot of peppermint schnapps with a beer chaser, not some after-dinner drink. It was hard getdown music for boogie and spew, the soundtrack that accompanied real high school life; its sole appeal and focus was the if-you're-not-with-me-you're-against-me universe where peer group rules were the only rules. Neatly sidestepped was the question of how "peers" and peer group were defined. Ironically, these new critics substituted one restrictive and onerous code of behavior for another; presumably it was okay because it was their own (more easily to niche-market, my dear).

The writers who knew better and could write well—like the late Lester Bangs, one of the prime exponents and martyrs to this ideology—purposely "dumbed down" their writing to fit into the new *zeitgeist* of the "doper" mentality, the peer group culture that defined itself in terms of style and the status of consumer goods, whose limited world revolved exclusively around getting loaded and partying. It was the "doper" culture of the seventies that in time transmuted itself into the yuppie culture of the eighties, which defined themselves in the same ways but with more expensive goods and designer drugs. What the music did in the present tense was more important than what it had said or was capable of saying within a larger cultural context since there effectively wasn't any, only a series of musical *nows* readily consumed and just as readily discarded until another *now* came along to replace it—fashion incarnate.

As championed by the *Creem* school, this "people's music," which eschewed literate criticism, reflected a basic meat-and-potatoes approach, heavily relying on sheer electric wattage, preferably a 10-foot stack of Marshall amps. The leading proponents for high-energy rock and roll came out of the Midwest: Iggy Pop, now a grandfather of the punk movement in the nineties,* and the MC5, the ideological poster band for the

---

*In 1969 the author asked Jim Osterberg, known now as Iggy Pop, who his favorite composers were. "Carl Orff, Richard Wagner, and Chuck Berry," he replied. His music still sounds like that.

White Panthers Party (WPP), a self-styled liberation rock and roll collective whose emphasis was more on "party" than *party.* Aside from its flashy graphic sense and a couple of house bands like The Frost and The Up, WPP offered no coherent social programs to speak of (or if it did, no one was never straight enough to carry the programs out). It was brainchild of John Sinclair, a radical community organizer and poet whose only all-purpose ideology was—wait for it, "Sex, drugs, and rock and roll."

Like the Black Panther Party on which it was loosely modeled, the official WPP motto was "All power to the people," despite the fact that the "people" only represented one segment of the population, one taste, and one point of view: rock's version of Socialist Realism. But the MC5 had their 15 minutes of fame before self-destructing. By the early seventies WPP had succeeded in making such a media commotion that the FBI put them on a watch list. Their de facto Minister of Information, Pun Plamandon, even briefly appeared on the Bureau's Most Wanted List, an event that conclusively proved just how out of touch the FBI was during that period. Poor Pun—while fleeing the clutches of the FBI, he was unceremoniously busted for littering in the Upper Michigan Peninsula. So much for revolutionary acts, but that's another story entirely.

When Grand Funk Railroad, a power trio of guitar, bass, and drums, literally blasted out of the Midwest onto the charts, knocking the critical establishment out of their seats with their raw power, the mind/body split between the Midwest and the East and West coast critics was revealed for all to see. Lead guitarist Mark Farner, long on power chords but short on technique, spearheaded the assault, flashily bludgeoning his primarily teenage, male working-class audience into submission on his way up the pop charts.

When the critics on the coasts got their hearing back, they were appalled and tried to smother the band in a blanket of bad reviews and scathing commentary. Terry Knight, the band's manager, far more in touch with the ways of the "real" commercial world as it was—not as the critics would have liked it to be— struck back. Craftily, he exploited the issue of the critics' "elitism" by taking out full-page ads in all the major music magazines and music trades that quoted some of the more savage reviews and juxtaposed the concert and record gross sales numbers beside them.[4] His media counterattack neatly deflected the whole issue away from the band toward the critics, using the old high school ploy of "us versus them," normal kids versus stodgy grown-ups. One enterprising writer of the "old school" neatly sidestepped the issue entirely by writing about the audience instead of the band; it was a far more revealing approach for those who were willing to read between the lines, and some did.

Though Grand Funk Railroad eventually receded on the charts, it was obvious that the market spoke with a louder voice; who was buying and in what numbers were far more crucial than analysis. Since the market ruled, critics were persuaded to review the market instead of the music. Maybe "art rock" had become too expensive to manufacture and distribute, to mount for the public, but the short version was that the "people's critics" deemed it too pretentious for the jus' plain folks to digest. The official line here has been disseminated forever after by Ellen Willis, one of the first women writers on rock and roll culture:

> At best [art rock] stimulated a vital and imaginative eclecticism
> that spread the values of rock and roll even as it diffused and di-
> luted them. At worst it rationalized a form of cultural upward
> mobility, concerned with achieving the appearance and preten-
> sions of art rather than the reality—the point being to "improve"
> rock and roll by making it palatable to the upper middle class.
> Either way it submerged rock and roll in something more amor-
> phous and high-toned called rock.[5]

However it's sliced, diced, and textured these days, the result effectively enshrined the commonly mistaken adolescent notion (though not necessarily restricted to that age group) that *all criticism* was ipso facto negative and "elitist" and so must be avoided at all costs. Any other posture ensured the label of

"class traitor," though ironically the best thing about rock and
roll up to that time had been that it *didn't* have such restrictive
class distinctions and appealed to a broader sociocultural base
instead of being circumscribed by the vagaries of teenage taste
and fad fashion—"no fun, my babe, no fun," as Iggy Pop might
have said. Instead, focusing on the continuities that held culture
together, the critics embraced the commerce that manipulated
and thrived on apparent cultural discontinuities. Swiftly, the art
was excised from the art criticism (that ability to exercise selective discernment), so that music (or film or literature, for that
matter) had to fit the specific ideological criteria of the market.
To attempt to praise an album with faint damns would only so-
licit audience incomprehension, getting in the way of the ultimate question: Should I buy it or not?

Thus this market-driven aesthetic forced cultural critics to
function as a either record company cheerleaders and publicists
at worst or savvy aesthetic handicappers who merely provided
consumer guides at best (as Robert Christgau did then and continues to do today). Though it made publisher/industry relations
smoother, there was also the chance for abuse on the part of the
record companies. Having made a substantial investment with
full-page ads on "the next big thing," the companies naturally
wanted to maximize their chances of success, regardless of the
"aesthetics" involved, as we have previously seen.[6] To be truthful,
this made some sort of mutated sense, since this payola scheme,
the manipulation of the marketplace by strategic infusions of
cash and other goods to influence sales of the product, was what
"the biz" had always been about, even when there was comparatively less money at stake. "Look, I'm subsidizing this magazine,"
the companies said in so many words, "at least cut us some
slack," just like large advertisers in major magazines do today (or
what newspaper editors say to rein in their arts critics from
teeing off on marginal or questionable products when advertising revenues are at stake). And of course the consumer/lis-
tener was the loser in this scheme, though no one said so at the
time.

Still it would be false to characterize all industry/critic relationships this way, for within the system there was a core of
publicists and company people who relied on critics with integrity who weren't just whores out for whatever goodies and
access they could get; the publicists depended on the occa-
sional reality check missing in their personal work environment,
too. It was an anticipated treat for this minority to spend some
part of their day, over lunch preferably, talking to someone who
had a working brain with an informed opinion attached, who
thought of the music business within a larger context than just
the old commercial in/out.

As for those good game players, this system worked just
fine, and those who came along, went along, and after a while,
one did get the feeling that he or she was doing God's work
(whatever that work happened to be and whatever was Number
1 on the charts). One could eventually be convinced after a
while, like John Rockwell, former rock critic at *The New York
Times*, that "commercial success doesn't so much attest to
quality as corroborate it; if you like something the millions like,
their general enthusiasm adds resonance to your private enthusiasm, certifying its universality."[7]

The downside of this happy new little reformulated world
was that eventually critics felt like they were in a caucus race. No
matter how hard they worked, they were always behind, snowed
under by the product to be reviewed, analyzed, and pigeon-
holed. If one perchance took a break, the backlog was a killer. It
was not unheard of for critics, while nibbling free hors d'oeuvres
at record company functions in the major markets and cities, to
informally compare notes on the latest releases and collectively
broker a consensus about the groups. If one was hip to the
dance, one could just see the ripple effect from these unofficial
rating sessions in various newspapers and music magazines in reviews that reflected similar approaches and sometimes even
used the same adjectives. One writer of the author's acquain-
tance dealt with the release glut by simply taking whatever

recordings had come in the morning's mail, putting them all on
automatic changer, and going about her business—cleaning,
filing, researching, making phone calls, whatever. If she stopped
what she was doing, she'd replay the cut; if she liked the cut,
she'd replay the whole side, and if that went well, she'd review
the album. The remainder she'd either archive to her collection,
save for her friends who liked "that kind" of music, or leave in a
pile by the door for anyone who came over to paw through and
sell for a buck a pop. Some days she made a buck.

Being privy to all kinds of inside information because of
special access to the managers, artists, or prerelease test press-
ings posed even tougher burdens for critics. Living in a state of
cultural fast-forward 3 to 5 months ahead of the general record-
buying public made critics cynical and isolated them from their
audience. After a while, like it or not, instead of being commentators on the business, they became an integral part of it
themselves, and that world weariness inevitably leaked into the
writing, killing spontaneity. It was way too much of a good
thing.

Of course, inside access could produce other ethical
dilemmas: Critic Patricia Kennealy, the editor of *Jazz and Pop,*
not only had a torrid love affair but actually married Jim Morrison of the Doors. Once their romance had begun, she found
it increasingly impossible to write objectively about the group
without using her inside knowledge or letting anyone know she
had it (or was having him). To compensate, she became rather
harsh in her public reviews of the group, going so far as to
lecture the Lizard King in print on his understanding of Wordsworth's *Preface to the Lyrical Ballads*—Morrison had published some of his desultory poetry and, like the editor herself,
had, as the song goes, "been through all F. Scott Fitzgerald's
books." Was this not part of his poetic education, she reasoned?
(Admittedly this could only have happened back then, since
these days the words of Wordsworth are probably used as
doorstops, if at all, by the general rock audience.)

Apart from the violation of their privacy, general knowledge of this affair within the music business would have proved not only problematic to Morrison (marrying a critic may be a novel way to get good notices, but it would not have been smiled upon in many quarters even then) but disastrous to Kennealy's own credibility as an objective journalist, though such ethical dilemmas are of little import today, precisely because the boundaries between news and publicity are either indistinct or nonexistent: A rock critic and rock star engaging in the same situation these days would certainly find themselves voluptuously spread all over the gossip pages and, equally certain, would be thrilled to bits to be there.

Twenty-eight years ago, it was a different story: To navigate around and through this quandary, Kennealy enlisted the help of a good friend, a former lover, to act as her escort, her "beard" at public functions, encouraging inquiring minds to think that she was otherwise engaged and effectively enabling her to carry on her relationship with the Lizard King while he had some modicum of personal privacy out of the public eye.[8] (The Morrisons were by no means the only transprofessional couple that rock and roll hath joined together and even conflict of interest could not put asunder—then as now, bedfellows make strange politics.)

Some critics crossed completely over the line, like Jon Landau, who became Bruce Springsteen's producer and manager in the seventies, but while he was doing so, he never wrote about the Boss for the press. Others formed their own bands, like R. Meltzer's Soft White Underbelly, or Robert Palmer's Insect Trust. Some became record producers, forswearing criticism entirely. Those within record companies wrote under other names, and the band played on.

By the midseventies, those who survived the cut eventually reached the point where the thrill was gone. They had become bored with business as usual, and who could blame them—it was getting to be the Disco Age after all. And boredom, as any reader of philosopher Søren Kierkegaard, the true Melancholy Dane, knows well, leads to a pack of trouble (basic riff: God was bored so He created Adam; Adam was bored so Eve was created for him; then Adam and Eve were bored ensemble so Cain and Abel were created for them both; and so on down the line). The critics (who'd learned their lessons from the Grand Funk debacle a few years before), instead of trashing the music that was making pots and pots of money for the industry, decided to create their own counterrevolution if only as a way to reassert their authority and promote their own canon—their favorite New York and Los Angeles underground bands that the industry had ignored. (The invention of the Seattle-based Grunge scene is a more recent example.)

As had happened a decade earlier, the English music scene, that bellwether for trends and a constant font of inspiration, if not fashion sense, came to the rescue with the punk rock movement,[9] a music and a performance style that expressed rage against the disco movement, raging inflation, and massive unemployment among working-class youth. Its raw, in-your-face style in expressing its rage—its very artlessness, in fact—appealed not only to the predominantly middle-class musicians who made up the strictly uncommercial New York and Los Angeles underground music scenes but also to critics looking for a good meaty critical hook.

49

English punk's celebration of unconsciousness, with its emphasis on hard drug, alcohol, and amphetamine use by musicians and audiences alike and wretched excesses in general (puking and spitting on the audience in particular), as well as the air of riot and physical danger that enveloped performances, was just the kind of style outrage that would bust open the smug plasticity of the disco world. It was hoped that punk would make music honest and authentic again—and cut a piece of the consumer pie for the bands involved, of course. Though no Americans had a clue as to what it felt like to be an unemployed working-class youth in England faced with truly no hope, the next best thing, they reasoned, if only perhaps to show some cultural solidarity, was to expropriate the performance style of the English working-class bands, along with their slang and dress, which was being hyped by the English fashion press.

Though it made a big media splash in New York and Los Angeles for a time, punk was a commercial failure, an imitation of reality with virtually no substance to it other than as a fashion statement. When inevitably funneled through music culture magazines from *Rolling Stone* on down into the great teenage heartland of America, an imitation of an imitation of reality, punk had its second life. As an urban legend, it was enthusiastically translated and reduced down to a style of dress and an attitude, like being a "hippie" or "jock" a behavioral shorthand armor plate that kids used to navigate through the teenage wasteland of American high school life.

Having been characterized as a radical cultural text for the forever after, punk in its time was little more than an attempt by a small group of artists and musicians to dominate the music scene and to substitute for the prevailing commercial sense one of their own liking. That the punk movement has today achieved a mythic state in the minds of cultural historians not only shows ignorance of what the music business was about then and continues to be about now but also overlooks how teenagers view music as a vehicle for their own self-expression, a temporary expedient that confuses style with substance in today's world, yet another example of adolescence's need to be different and shocking for the sake of being different and shocking.

"It wasn't political," stated Legs McNeil, the editor of *Punk* magazine 20 years later. "I mean, maybe that is political. I mean the great thing about punk was that it had no political agenda. It was about real freedom, personal freedom. It was also about doing anything that's gonna offend a grown-up. Just being as of-

fensive as possible. Which seemed delightful, just euphoric."[10]
Punk wasn't a statement of working-class solidarity either,

> it was about advocating kids to not wait to be told what to do,
> but live for themselves, it was about trying to get people to use
> their imaginations again, it was about not being perfect, it was
> about saying it was okay to be amateurish and funny, that real
> creativity came out of making a mess, it was about working with
> what you got in front of you and turning everything embar-
> rassing, awful and stupid in your life to your advantage.[11]

There was nothing revolutionary about this position, and if the truth be known, whoever has somehow survived being an adolescent can attest to similar feelings whatever age or era. Mc-Neil is exercising his 20/20 hindsight now that middle age is staring him in the face. He was also neither a musician nor an artist but a clubbie/observer. The real artists checked out of punk as rapidly as they had checked into it. Far from being some kind of radical restatement, the punk movement was a conservative return to the traditional needs of youth to be different at any cost, purely for the sake of being different. A further extension of the *Creem* school ethos 5 years later, it was a mannered self-conscious turning-away from any realization of the limitless possibilities of what music could be and do, not for one segment of the population but for everyone. In truth, punk was a second-generation imitation of the pop art scene that Andy Warhol mined, but it was based on a distorted reflection absorbed into mainstream American culture, there to be consumed by the middle-class suburban teenagers for whom it was intended.

By the end of the seventies, in a little over a decade, what had been music for people of all ages had been turned into exclusively the music of youth, one more market that fluctuates every 2 to 4 years. This was due to the law of generations, which was succinctly described by the historian Gilbert Ostrander:

> The younger generation is at all times simultaneously appearing
> on the field and moving off the field and trying to stay on the
> field while turning into something else. No sooner have the rules

of the game been officially explained by the younger generation,
than another game is discovered to be in progress on the same
field under different rules by a somewhat different younger generation.[12]

So it goes in the music business these days. The rock and
roll world is no longer the property of just one particular group
of teenagers from a specific time and place; it is a pliant
metaphor that every succeeding generation uses as it sees fit for
its own needs. Though it speaks in many rhythms, it no longer
does so in a common tongue, for each *now* has a specialized
constituency with its media organs and consumer goods, its
own sociology and secret handshakes. Who controls the generations and speaks for them has given rise to bloody turf wars
within the halls of academe.

While these battles rage, the common context in which all
these musics speak to each other and to us has been irretriev-
ably lost. This loss has lead to a remarkable form of cultural myopia where the rock and roll world has become all there is, a
realm where Michael Jackson's sexual proclivities, or lack of
same, or Madonna's status as a pop icon are considered news to
be treated seriously by public media and academia instead of
the public relations ploys they are, where fashion is news and
news is fashionable. More's the pity because rock and roll's alternative vision was potentially far more all-encompassing, less
exclusive, and less frightening than the specter of losing status
in high school—which seems to the preoccupation of most
Americans, if we believe our media. This myopia not only is diminishing our collective sense of self but is well on the way to
devouring the world in which we live. Our focus has been nar-
rowed, as Ed Ward has observed with ample justification:

> Hey, the poets of our time are poets, not rock lyricists; the musi-
> cians who will leave the mark are musicians, not rock musicians;
> the story-tellers of our time are writing fiction and journalism,
> not rock criticism; the important artists of our time are artists,
> not rock artists. If their lives or works of art touch rock and roll,

well and good, and damn near unavoidable, but please don't confuse cause and effect, form and content, or structure and meaning. There's a big wide world out there—don't you want to know about it?[13]

Who Stole the Bomp from the Bomp Sha Bomp? We did, and all because we've allowed ourselves to be convinced that the music that inhabits our lives is no longer a forum for larger issues, but exists as hostage to youthful nostalgia, an extraordinarily useful commercial tool.

Chapter 3

Blame It on the Sixties

"The style of your own time is always invisible," and if it's not, it's fake.[1]

Headache

When I first heard the song "Revolution" by the Beatles in 1969, I never thought 20 years later it would be used to sell sneakers. I suppose one shouldn't be shocked at progress, at an evolution natural in this commercial society, though it does seem a perverse example of an environmentally friendly method of recycling outdated cultural resources. Yet even if the commercial totally decontextualized the song, it didn't seem to tick off anyone—save for a few old sixties soreheads—and for the most part, it was just another Nike campaign that came and went.

Perhaps.

At the same time, virtually no one seems to have remarked on how smoothly and seamlessly hip-hop and rap, the current generation's style and fashion, have made a similar transition to the commercial sphere, their *zeitgeist* speedily adapted and expropriated to sell everything from jeans to kid's toys. Perhaps music might not mean the same thing to this generation or have the same cultural significance as rock and roll did in the sixties, or more to the point, unlike those old soreheads, maybe this generation is just more accepting of the peculiarly American truism that whatever starts out "on the corner" will eventually wind up selling something and cash in on it. Isn't it a potent testament to the continued power of the American dream that even the casualties of it "buy in"?

"It's just a song, isn't it?" asks the new generation in the process of struggling to define itself. Anyway, what do those sixties guys have to complain about? Aren't the sixties back big time, even if it's a caricature? Mini-skirts are vogue, the acid/X rave scene is happening, just like the psychedelic days of yore, man. It's sex, drugs, and rock and roll all over again, or still—MTV broadcasts rock and roll videos and news 24 hours a day and has its own shopping network and even a Washington correspondent; isn't that what it was all about?

Everybody's socially conscious—there's even an environmentally safe automobile antifreeze on the market, something that won't harm the environment or the dog if it happens to lap it up. And haven't all those sixties therapies been validated and mainstreamed in the nineties? Shiatsu, acupuncture, rolphing, past life regression therapy, and vitamin therapies of all kinds are listed right there in the *Yellow Pages*. What you don't find in the catalogues you can test-drive at New Age conventions in any large regional mall these days; check the Internet for times and places, everybody's doing it now. What did Wavy Gravy, that archetypal sixties Merry Prankster say at the 30th anniversary of the 1964 Free Speech Movement in Berkeley, California? "The nineties are the sixties reversed?" Numerologically speaking, he may be right, but there's more to it than that, much more.

For some, a highly tangible and significant sign of the domination of sixties' ideology in the nineties was the 1992 election of William Jefferson Clinton as the 41st President of the United States, a man who, during the presidential campaign, admitted that as a college student not only did he protest against the war and legally avoid the draft, but he also experimented with drugs. Clinton quickly qualified this revelation by adding that although he may have smoked a little dope in college, like everyone else of his generation, he "did not inhale," which seemed to make matters all right again—or perhaps slightly worse, as though he tried it yet didn't try it.* Currently an innergenerational in-joke, that kind of public confession would have been unthinkable a mere decade ago when a highly (sorry!) qualified candidate for the Reagan Supreme Court was rejected because of a similar youthful folly at Harvard Law.

Clinton's election parallels what has come to cap the full ascendence to power in colleges and universities of many former anti-War activists (careerists and opportunists alike) who survived and were influenced by the issues of those times. For the ultraleft politically correct fringe the revolution hasn't gone far enough, while from the point of view of knee-jerk old woman conservative critics, most prominently Allan Bloom, far too much damage has already been done. For him, these radicals' dubious "contributions" have the faint odor of a self-promoting nostalgia, the consequence of finally coming to terms with "growing up," itself a self-serving rationalization for becoming another kind of invidious "establishment," rigid as the one they'd hoped to overthrow when they were mere children. "What remains," Bloom acidly observes,

> is a certain self-promotion by people who took part in it all, now in their forties, having come to terms with the "establishment"

---

*Historical note: When Bill Clinton was at Oxford, hashish was the drug of choice because it was cost-effective and plentiful; marijuana wasn't widely available, and if it was, it was prohibitively expensive. Hash was ingested by either smoking it in a pipe or mixing crumbles of it with loose cigarette tobacco; the mixture was rolled into a spliff (a hashish joint made up of anywhere from three to six cigarette papers and held together with a cardboard mouthpiece, itself a work of art). However it was consumed, the smoke was harsh. If one inhaled it like a regular cigarette, one ran the risk of coughing oneself silly. Instead one developed the technique of swallowing amounts in small gulps, i.e., *not inhaling*, as everyone who survived the sixties in some form or other knows well. Thus the line "did not inhale" doesn't mean that he was squeamish and not really there with it, though more to the point, it would be far more unusual for anyone of that generation *not* to have inhaled at least once for curiosity's sake, which was the point lost in the translation. To be sure, it just wasn't the act as much as what went on "inside" during the act. All heads weren't created equal. Stay tuned.

but dispersing a nostalgic essence in the media, where, of course, many of them are flourishing, admitting that it was unreal but asserting that it was a moment of significance.[2]

I suspect that even Allan Bloom knew in his heart of hearts that the sixties was no mere "moment of significance" in the order of things or else he wouldn't have fulminated about the legacies of the sixties so eloquently and passionately in his book, *The Closing of the American Mind.* But as the title of Simone Signoret's biography suggests, "Nostalgia just ain't what it used to be," not only for conservatives like Bloom but also for sixties apologists like Todd Gitlin and boosters, who have expropriated the external trappings elaborated in brief here. Both sides seemed to have ignored the era's abundant and transcendent inner essences, rituals, and maps that made that time if not unique, then at least historically resonant with echoes of earlier periods in American cultural history.

According to Fred Davis, a sociologist who has studied the phenomenon, contemporary history itself is in danger of becoming a victim of nostalgia, which he defines as

> one of the means—or better, one of the more readily accessible psychological lenses—we employ in the never ending work of constructing, maintaining, and reconstructing our identities . . . it can be thought of as a kind of telephoto lens on life which, while it magnifies and prettifies some segments of our past, simultaneously blurs and grays other segments, typically those closer to us in time.[3]

Contemporary cultural history is continually being filtered through the fast-forward world of fashion and commerce, where, in its search for the new in the old, nothing appears to be what it is or indeed was, where all is product. To Davis, nostalgia's function is that it

> mediates the selection, distillation, refinement, and integration of these scenes, events, personalities, attitudes, and practices from the past that make an identifiable generation of what

would otherwise remain a featureless demographic cohort, eg.
the Edwardians, the jazz age generation, the children of the depression, the silent generation and the turned-on generation.[4]

Since there is this continual need for new product in this
hyped-up system, "the very objects of collective nostalgia are in
themselves media creations from the recent past. In other
words, in their ceaseless search for new marketable objects of
nostalgia, the media now do little but devour themselves."[5] Consequently, Americans are never sure what they are being nostalgic about because the ideas themselves are always being
rewritten and reinterpreted to suit the "myopia of the moment"
dictated by fashion. Is the American past akin to an antique
chair, table, rug, or armoire, at least 100 years old according to
the dictionary, or to an Andy Warhol "collectible" cookie jar, a
bit of manufactured kitsch from the forties or fifties? Or does it
lie in the idealized never-never realm of classical Greece, as
Allan Bloom and his cohorts believe, in a past can be only imperfectly grasped through its reinterpreted texts?

61

Or none of the above? For what we propose to do here, as
anthropologist Clifford Geertz suggests, is instead of "looking
behind the interfering glosses that connect us [looking] *through*
them."[6] When we do, it appears that the sixties has become a ca-
sualty, homogenized out of recognition and Cheesewhizzed by
market forces and media.

True, the surface manifestations—sex, drugs, and rock and
roll, protest and mini-skirts—are with us still and were noted by
news media then, but there was far more going on that has been
effectively ignored and/or misreported because it didn't suit the
needs of hot copy[7]—but then again, some things change little.
Davis's full court field theory to the contrary, the sixties was not
another "featureless demographic cohort," for demographers
have noted that its greatest impact came with the explosion of students in high school. In the 1930s the ratio of 14- to 17-year-olds in
high school had passed 50%, by the 1950s that number had risen

to 73% (when the term "teenager" was coined), and by the mid-sixties, all but 5% of the teenage population was in high school.

When college was factored in and the age when one normally entered the workplace was pushed up to 21 or 22, this indicated, according to Landon Y. Jones in *Great Expectations*, that "America's largest generation was growing up in an age-segregated universe, cut off from outside society and . . . bound together by their own prolonged adolescence."[8] But it wasn't just the numbers as much as what could be done with them—and what was.

Indeed, before one starts blaming the sixties for the supposed mess it has made of the nineties—what with the welfare crisis, the vicious gender battles in the political correctness arena, the rise of AIDS, affirmative action, the overregulation of the environment, drive-by shootings, and youth running wild in the streets (a continuing saga, as any social historian knows)—it would be well to determine just exactly what comprised that decade. What visions, illuminations, epiphanies, insights, what dialectical discussions were bubbling underneath the surface of this outsized adolescent population that the media began to promote? We need therefore to explore, in the Melvilleian sense, the "whiteness of the whale" that was the sixties and that exists now only in fashion-directed memory. And if it's all about nostalgia, let's at least attempt to be nostalgic about the right things, about Beatniks and Heads,* hippies and dopers (proto-

---

*The term "Head" is used in that peculiarly sixties sense to mean one who had assimilated the spoken, sung, and seen (i.e., the great art and ideas of all our times) and who understood that cosmic dance and laughter, and with that awareness, acted on what one found in those altered states of consciousness. After having absorbed the lessons from all those archetypal visions of morality, philosophy, and cosmology, heads tried to live their lives accordingly in the belief that this life is but a transition into the next, that the wheel of karma turns for all whether they know it or not. And if one is truly aware of all those things, one had no choice *except* to act on what one knew, because *not acting* on that (having reached that level of awareness to see all those things) meant returning to the wheel to try to get it right next time instead of evolving to a Being of Light.

typical yuppies with a lower grade of goods), for that was what it was all about during those 20 years from the midfifties to the early seventies. Although everyone eventually went on the trip, like Pablo's Magic Circus in Hermann Hesse's *Steppenwolf*, it was "For Madmen Only. Not for Everybody. Price of Admission Your Mind." Come. Let's go.

Fragments from "The Book of Head"

"Heads" were primarily a literate, enlightened, and informed elite who saw a higher spiritual reality beyond the annual homecoming game of fifties team America while they were spectators in it. They kept a low profile, were almost invisible except that they read for a variety of experience: *Steppenwolf, The Brothers Karamazov, Waiting for Godot, On the Road, The Waste Land, Howl:* young and old in the tradition pieced the cultural mosaic together. "Beats" suffered and strived in the shadows of *The Lonely Crowd* and *The Organization Man*. The distance between Beats and Heads was incalculable; Heads assimilated all their information moving into, not away from, the world, without the uniform: the black turtleneck and all that jazz.

Beat.

Beats were cool cynics who sneered at the agency schnorrers chained to the monotonous beat of the 8:30 from Bridgeport. You couldn't be cool and dig on your work—that's lame, man. The only thing the Beats dug was their alienation, which they deified. Beats embraced jazz and abstract expressionism; to get the most out of jazz you had to be cool, detached, uninvolved. Digging mystical abstract expressionism was like listening to Bird, 'Trane, or Miles—interiors that lead to other interiors.

Beats hiply and coolly manifested their lifestyle as if their appearance and attitude alone would blow the Squares away (like post '67 counterculture and subsequent stylistic permutations thereafter). Heads were interior but aware. Beats were exterior and insular. Jazz and folk. Jazz is a metaphor on a metaphor of black alienation. Folk blues is the story of that alienation itself, the struggle, a musical social history. Beats talked too much, reacting against psychoanalysis by becoming their own walking traumas. Heads saw Beat angst as self-limiting and self-imposed and probed their own universal unconscious.

Heads explored interior spaces freely, constrained by no intellectual viewpoint, open to a multiplicity. Intellectual eclectics, they viewed knowledge as a totality of information, a joyous cosmology, a synthesis used to understand *the universe*, by knowing what things are composed of, motivated by, influenced by. Only when you begin to see the totality of knowledge can you transcend your environment.

Head. Either you were or you weren't. You could spot them on the street since they possessed an inner animation, their brains radiated energy. Heads were not cool—cool was a hipster affectation. Cool was the Beat form of transcendence; but it was pure selfishness, a self-image, an attitude you struck, a pose. Hipsters and Beats were forever concerned about their cool, it was their religion—like Pynchon's Stencil in *V*, whose motto was "Keep cool but care," only the Beats never did care. To be cool with yourself meant being largely uninvolved with the world at large. Heads were never uninvolved: Though they may have possessed cool heads, it was their manner.

Heads integrated realities—POP. Like Claes Oldenburg's plastic hamburgers. Getting to the marrow of an experience: POP. Reality is made up of contradictions, trompe l'oeil, slapstick, Marx Brothers, surrealistic moments. Time is funny, not your individual place in it. Your perspective makes it funny, in time *intime*. Plastic lipstick holders, plastic food—the perfect commercial object, the perfect commercial—POP.

America is one big commercial wasteland, T. S. Eliot without the footnotes. The Beats called it the Square Life; solipsistic Steppenwolves, they fled on the road, to North Beach, Greenwich Village, Seattle, come on, let's go, they said. Beats thought if they ignored time it would cease to exist; the gray fifties would vanish like cigarette haze in the Five Spot. Heads knew it wouldn't. Why run? One builds and lives within an ever-expanding continuum; besides, awareness is immanent for everyone, in time. America was waiting for awareness, had been since its creation.

Head consciousness was self-reflexive and universal, while the Beats deified the addict. Heroin was the ultimate Beat trip, a chemically induced existentialism, and the junkie was Christ crucified and grooving on celestial oblivion of smack. The Square Life could be shut out for good that way. Get back, get under, get out of it; later for that they said. No wonder Bird lived in Beatsville.

Drugs were not a necessary part of the Head cosmology, though they later assumed preeminence when Head culture was debased, brokered as a commodity, media-eclipsed to "hippie." Drugs were an aid to attaining and integrating knowledge, one way to build up experience, but not the only way. (Timothy Leary, the High Priest of LSD, was a psychedelic salesman who sold out into street time, snake oil for the soul.) Drugs that expanded the consciousness instead of insulating it were prized and revered—grass, hashish, psychedelics didn't take you "out of it" but "into it." Heads felt that people who depended on depressants (tranquilizers, barbiturates, heroin, or alcohol) were inferior, low energy, their priorities and human potentialities limited because they preferred oblivion to enlightenment.

Drugs 100 years ago were heady metaphors, a peculiar kind of gateway for Zenos Clark, a friend of William James, whose letter was quoted in his *Varieties of Religious Experience:*

So the present is already a foregone conclusion, and I am ever too late to understand it. But at the moment of recovery from anesthetics [ether], just then, before starting on life, I catch, so to speak, a glimpse of my heels, a glimpse of the eternal process just in the act of starting. The truth is that we travel on a journey that was accomplished before we set out; and the real end of philosophy is accomplished, not when we arrive at, but when we remain in, our destination (being already there)—which may occur vicariously in this life when we cease our intellectual questioning.[9]

They were still doing that, catching "a glimpse" into the forties, although mescaline, not ether, provided the charge, just as Aldous Huxley wrote in 1954 in *The Doors of Perception* for a continuous transcendent metaphor. In the sixties LSD was another expanding intellectual metaphor that forced you to keep your mind pliant whereby those trips and mental excursions will take you all sorts of places you want to go. Knowledge is what it's all about, Alfie. Timeslides cause cosmic laughter where Harry Haller becomes The Outsider. Pablo's Magic Theater presents the possibilities of the untrammeled mind; you can get "out of it" but you never get "away from it."

The funniest thing Abbie Hoffman ever said was, "The only dope worth shooting is Nixon." He wasn't far from wrong. Drugs in America, drugs and America, had been part and parcel of the psychic landscape for more than 100 years for better or worse, a patent medicine prime ingredient. Cocaine and marijuana were big in the twenties. Jazz and tea, stick, reefer all went together in the Beat scene. The hipster smoked pot to dig on his alienation, to enjoy his cool jazz. Some people burned themselves out, some people didn't; it was just there. Harry M. Anslinger, Federal Bureau of Narcotics Commissioner from the thirties to the fifties, declared marijuana "the destroyer of youth" and banned its over-the-counter sale. Like the "Noble Experiment," Prohibition, the ban encouraged organized crime and mass civil disobedience. By banning all "bad" drugs and controlling information on them, the government thought it would be able to keep people in line.

Couched in crude racist and sexist iconography, the fifties anti-drug campaign made no distinction between pushers and dealers. It was more than mere linguistics; the difference spanned and encapsulated cultures. Pushers were capitalists personified, in it for the money; their clients were addicted. In truth, dealers were folk heroes to the developing Head culture, an integral part of the community they served, not outlaws. The drugs they sold were consciousness-expanding and nonaddictive. They linked communities together with input and communications. Unlike the oblivion sellers in William S. Burroughs' *Naked Lunch* who'd peddle baby powder or Saniflush, only one step ahead of the police, psychedelic dealers were concerned about their friends and the purity of their goods. Dealers never sold LSD to people they didn't like or trust. They'd say, "What are you going to use this for and where are you going to use it, and with whom?" Long ago and far, far away.

With or without drugs Heads sought a cross-cultural ecological intellectual overview, where ecology was the study of the natural interdependence of systems, a basic organizing principle. For instance, to the Head it naturally made no sense to manufacture an automobile that fell apart in 2 years. It was more economical in the long run to produce a low-maintenance, high-performance vehicle. Though a highly reasonable position, this attitude/outlook was also highly subversive to the American businessmen, the promise of GE's All-Electric Kitchen as sold by future President Ronald Reagan on TV's *Death Valley Days*. Instead of a state of dependence, Heads strove to develop themselves to the highest self-actualizing state possible. It was a foregone conclusion: Heads were enemies of the state; was there any doubt of it?

Freedom was the constant. Free your mind—everyone has civil rights, all races and creeds, individuals as well as nations (collections of interconnected communities, social polities); lunchcounter sit-ins, freedom rides for voter registration, or Ban the Bomb marches all encompassed similar aims. Civil rights went along with civic duty and individual responsibility to participate in the decisions of government as well as a collective responsibility by which American democracy allegedly maintained itself. Thus, the war in Vietnam was a massive and disgraceful violation of the civil rights of the individuals in country and out, just as representative of the state of the union as the bus burnings in Americus, Georgia.

The publication of *The Pentagon Papers* brought home for all to see the realization that Dr. Strangelove, Henry Kissinger, and Harry M. Anslinger were one and the same, that civil rights also included freedom from being willfully and consciously misinformed by one's government about everything from drug toxicity to environmental damage, the fruits of the new American Way ("Plastics," The Graduate was advised). *Voila!* Plastic people, plastic culture. Beats accepted it all placidly, dropped out, tried the old end-around play while Heads did not; they dropped in, had to, no choice. The only way to go was straight ahead, to confront the Frankenstein monster that had been or was being created for teenage America.

Against the aural background of Tin Pan Alley, teenage ditties and made-for-order products for the burgeoning, assiduously cultivated, and statistic-driven new market were contrary and countervailing trends. A conscious search for authenticity, for roots, for an authentic indigenous organic cultural referent that spoke to the nascent sense of community, polity, and civil rights was brewing. The early-sixties urban folk revival was a natural springboard for these ideals, the resurgence of humanism in an inhuman era overshadowed by the threat nuclear warfare. Pete Seeger (with or without the Weavers), Ewan McCall, Jean Redpath, Cisco Houston, the Greenbriar Boys—all spurred the reexamination of those marginalized and crushed by Team America like the American hobo and the rural poor of Appalachia. Their songs raised questions about social issues that had been overlooked. For them and other troubadours, the essential American experience was Delta or Chicago-style electric blues, Muddy Waters or Nathan Beauregard, the music of the rural and urban disenfranchised, not the Tin Pan Alley product of Sinatra, Pattie Page, the Andrews Sisters, Perry Como. Time had come to take back control of the module of Spaceship America.

In 1963, along came the Beatles with an insistent electric energy that eventually fused with the American folk scene. Along went Bob Dylan, Simon and Garfunkel, and a host of other young folk performers, and the folk rock crossover—blues for white people to spread the word. Head consciousness flowered in its syncopated earthy rhythms and rhymes cobbled from the reading of Whitman, Dylan Thomas, and Joyce in music that produced literate multidimensional insights on and about time, all kinds.

Art time: Allen Kaprow. Art is a series of events that involve the spectator, an environment you can manipulate and freely pass through. The war in Vietnam was a blunder that turned into a happening that got out of control. Thank you again, Doctor Strangelove.

Understanding Media was the treatise of the age, the ultimate obviousness and obliviousness. McLuhan and Quentin Fiore demonstrated the results of image retention time. In 1966, hippies were the result of *Understanding Media.* In 1968, Yippies were the result of the understanding of *Understanding Media,* an imitation of an imitation of a reality that had been expressly manufactured. Andy Warhol in his pungent commercial cynicism transformed commercial soup cans into natural art statements by drawing the eye from the sublime to the ridiculousness of American culture. Camp/pop becomes Batman!, *Your Hit Parade* becomes *Shindig* and *Hullabaloo,* spangles a-go-go.

Head time has echoes forward and backward, like Antonioni's movie *Blow Up,* where when you dissolve reality you rediscover it anew where it's least expected, in random artifice like random photos. Reality is a chance photograph that becomes greater than the meaning of your life. You blow it up, eventually to become both the photo and the lab technician who creates it.

Head consciousness with Beatles/folk input becomes mod—Mary Quant, Twiggy, mini-skirts, Richard Lester's *The Knack*. Sets change and images flicker. People dance in strobe lights: syncopated movement images frozen while LBJ "wars" on poverty, a spectacular misnomer, and simultaneously escalates the war. Teach-ins on college campuses focus contemporary time on historical imperatives ignoring human nature in statistical manipulations. Fuck the war. What's the difference between *The Man from U.N.C.L.E.*, Maxwell Smart, and the CIA? (Not much, even now.) Traditional notions of "straight" historical time broke down, and a generation broke away.

Free the Indianapolis 500.

Media changes man by total immersion. Take Garroway's *Wide, Wide World*, mix with Murrow's *Person to Person*, multiply television sets as babysitters, and add Walter Cronkite. Media now makes artificial communities founded on media artifacts, TV trivia, flared, smoothed, wrinkle-free time, the all-nourishing manna.

McLuhan Oramus.

Truth? What can that be? It's relative, isn't it? said those drowning in a sea of commercial artifactual time. When you become the truth, or what you think the truth is, history and time become material for an eternal cartoon, just like R. Crumb Reality later in the decade said in reply.

Mister Goodbar says, "Go fuck yourself. Do it today!"

Right.

And if you're into truth, you're into movement ("the perfection of memory consisting, it would seem/in the never-to-be-completed," as Amy Clampitt wrote in her poem "Dancers Exercising"[10]), you must go back to history. You unearth it, rediscover it, relive it, you confront the evil therein (as well as the joy), which, though it can't be accepted, is acknowledged as omnipresent despite the governmental Anslingerian imperative that's it's bad for you to know. Time (and history) is a continuous show spanning aeons since cave was crack. Through consciousness of history (and time) you experience the continuum and shift inside from time to time, play with pieces of time, spaces in time you are or will be part of. Music is timeless, head music fused time signatures together, like a 12-tone serial version of "In the Midnight Hour" or a 4/4 Magnificat. The background music of your life some days could be *Parsival* or "Ain't Misbehaving," a Zuni war chant or a monkey chant from Bali.

Watching Everett Dirksen filibuster back in the sixties was no better or different than reading that older blusterer Cicero's *Against Cataline*. Politics continues to be entertainment, unfortunately. LBJ, Kennedy, Nixon, Cleon, Augustus, Justinian the Great, political time is always the same old time—who's to choose? The dude with that brunette looker you saw flashing down Sunset Strip or Park Avenue in the white Mercedes 450 used to be a regular at Maeceanus' house, remember?

Hiya Quintus.

Time (and history) is a weird parade. You're in it. It's happening.

So let's bring back Aristophanes.

He hasn't left.

Exactly, and here you are again.

Whether it's the slave markets or the baths or some con-
catenation of the two, it shouldn't be such a large mental
reach. Naturally to describe that place you have to invent a new
language or twist the possibilities—like E. E. Cummings,
Gertrude Stein, and James Joyce—of the one you have. When
you expand the peripheries of your ignorance to find knowledge, language extends with it. Young Robert Zimmermann
(Bob Dylan) extended the language of pop music, mixing
Kierkegaard, Beckett, Patchen, and Robert Frost with street-
fighting man and made it to Highway 61, where God said to
Abraham, "Kill me a son," and Abe said, "God, you must be
putting me on," and he (along with the rest of the generation)
grooved to the sounds of Little T. S. Eliot and the Imperials. If
all knowledge is continuous as understanding, use different
forms of language, pictures, sound. Transliterate the image. A
good light show is better than LSD if you're really there. Heads
opened themselves to the vision of the simultaneity of the
heavenly spheres, better than a McLuhanesque Madison Avenue celluloid joke.

Who's to choose?

Heads believed in a human and humane nation-state of
mind that transcended borders and political systems, that broke
down all ideologies because it was stronger and more direct,
that would, they hoped, finally destroy the myth that a man
does not live by ideology alone, but rather by a human integrity
that broke through and reordered ideologies. Heads believed in
the idea of humankind over U.S.A., that the only thing that
should be exploited is human potential, not avarice, greed, fear,
and its stepchildren war, famine, pestilence, and prejudice. So
how did this "land of the free and home of the brave" come to
be known as The Home Shopping Network?

If you believe people have energy, then it's possible to
want to exorcise the Pentagon of evil spirits and raise it off the
ground, or even stop the war with street theater, or believe in

magic. It's such a cartoon, this TV world. Turn off the sound and put on a Stones record, ferchrissakes.

This is your time, good time, bad time. You can get thrown in the hole or put yourself there. Your house is your castle, your prison, your body too, but your soul is immortal. It's all free time, old used time, time that is public domain. Heads check out the time before they play within it, and here's what happened when they did.

The Fragmented Head

> I say that our New World democracy, however great a success in uplifting the masses out of their sloughs, in materialistic development, producers, and in a certain highly deceptive superficial popular intellectuality, is, so far, an almost complete failure in its social aspects, and in really grand religious, moral, literary, and aesthetic results.
>
> WALT WHITMAN, *Democratic Vistas*[11]

> Conspiracy? We couldn't even agree on where to go to lunch.
> (attributed to Abbie Hoffman during the Chicago 7 Trial)

Only those ignorant of the sweep and texture of American history would attempt to pigeonhole the protest movement and the allied social activism that grew out of the sixties as mere exercises of youthful folly, the consequences of a demographic hiccough; to the contrary, protest—not violence—is as American as apple pie, and it has been woven into the texture of the American experience since the Boston Tea Party. But unlike the Boston Tea Party, the anti-War movement encompassed a far broader racial, social, and gender spectrum: men and women, young and old, rich and poor, black and white, World War II vets and war resisters, Quakers, Catholics, Jews, Protestants, Evangelicals, Atheists, clergymen, and politicians (though only a few and not until the wind was blowing favorably). That wave of discontent that exploded onto the pages of newspapers and cathode ray tubes in the late sixties had been bubbling in the minds of artists, philosophers, and social critics for over 100 years. What was unique in a sense was that the concerns for civil rights, the nature of representative democracy, all commingled into a metaphor of the war in Southeast Asia. Indeed the war wasn't a cause of the sixties; it was a symptom of what had been wrong with the country since the end of World War II. One hundred years or so ago, here's how Walt Whitman so eloquently described the ferment of American nation/spirit in *Democratic Vistas:*

> The problem, as it seems to me, presented to the New World, is, under permanent law and order, and after preserving cohesion, (ensemble-Individuality,) at all hazards, to vitalize man's free play of special Personalism, recognizing in it something that calls ever more to be considered, fed, and adopted as the substratum for the best that belongs to us, (government indeed is for it) including the new esthetics of our future.[12]

The silent vigils, sit-ins, and mass marches were all attempts to put into practice that Whitmanesque idea of "ensemble/individuality," to refocus on fundamental American values that had been lost in the post-World War II/Cold War economic abundance of the fifties. Far from being unpatriotic and anti-American, the variegated protest movement was motivated by "the best that belongs to us." It wasn't just "our war," as war had skipped every other generation in twentieth-century America, nor merely a *realpolitik* exercise in the Cold War chess game of international relations as the government cynically and antiseptically framed and packaged it: It was *the* defining metaphor, a bald-faced cynical manipulation and perversion of the American spirit that Whitman, Emerson, Thoreau, and other writers invoked when they spoke *to* and *for*, not *at*, the American soul.

The war in Vietnam merely exacerbated tensions already bubbling in America at home and served as a "bait-and-switch" technique to keep Americans from understanding and confronting the questions that Johnson's Great Society had imper-

fectly dealt with. Why were we fighting other people's wars of
liberation and sending all this military aid when our own
country was in need of it, when there was so much to do in
health, education, and the welfare of our citizens? Was our
stated commitment to freedom and democracy only for export?

Really, it's just business, forget that other stuff, said the mil-
itary-industrial complex, which, when the layers of obfuscation
and self-serving rhetoric were peeled away and its corporate reports were scrutinized by peace activist historians and economists, was revealed to be the engine that motored the American
economy and had been motoring it since the end of World War
II. The interlocking lattice of companies that fed the machine
turned out to be immense—everyone was directly or indirectly
involved. All of which eventually gave new meaning to the
aphorism coined by George Orwell in *1984* that "War is peace,"
which in the sixties itself was further extended in Kurt Vonnegut's *Cat's Cradle* to "Truth is lies," which was transmogrified
into a popular demo placard/slogan of the time: "War is good
business, invest your son." Is there a linkage between civil rights
and the War? Why was war the only economic engine that
could run America? Was the War also an arm of domestic social policy? Was that really possible? Why? This seems wrong,
we protest.

75

What are you guys, un-American? the authorities wanted
to know. What's wrong with providing well-paying jobs and full
employment for citizens—that's what we're supposed to do,
isn't it? Isn't that why our economic system is the envy of the
world?

In reality, the government was saying that being profligate
with American human and material resources really benefits
the average citizen, that human beings were a disposable element that the post-World War II "peace" created, that investing
in the future productivity of American citizens was of less marginal utility than smart bombs, napalm, and chemical defo-

liants. If Johnson had waged his "war" on poverty with the same single-minded allocation of resources that were expended in South Vietnam, poverty would have been eliminated. There was some kind of cracked logic at work that motivated the government to "protect" foreign civil rights while its own citizens weren't fully enfranchised—not cost-effective enough, eh? The war in Vietnam may have seemed to be good for business, but whose?

Question Authority? Which authority? Whose? The one that demonstrates mastery and competence? The one that looks out for the interests of *all* our citizens? Or only those who have a financial stake in the exercise? Question Authority? You bet your ass we do, replied the mothers and fathers, sons, daughters, grandfathers, grandmothers, the freedom marchers black and white, young and old who were starting to get the message. Why accept answers to our questions that are couched in dehumanizing technical jargon, whose meaning changes monthly (or weekly), an authority, which, when finally ratted out by the press through the leak of *The Pentagon Papers*, prosecutes the leaker to deflect criticism. Instead of answering your questions, we'll make *you* the enemy and thereby suppress all those embarrassing questions for which we have no good answers nor indeed adequate ones and avoid answering at all costs. "Question Authority" may have been a popular lapel button (now a collectible for sixties trivia specialists), but it was also one of the generation's defining ideologies that allied itself firmly with its past. What began with doubts about America's involvement in Vietnam inevitably had to end up in the total examination of the essential nature of the character of American democracy itself.

Unfortunately, as the sixties came to an end, the symbolism of Question Authority became debased and ultimately lost its meaty metaphorical resonances. Taking the query out of the "ensemble/individuality" arena, counterculture youth spokesmen reduced it to a generational question of style of "Don't Trust

Anyone over 30," a wiseass comeback and advertising gimmick that conclusively shut down the intergenerational dialogue about the nature of America that the War had finally opened up. It was a catchphrase coined by youth spokesman who were way over 30 themselves.[13]

It took almost 5 years for public protest to reach the point where Lyndon Johnson declined to run for a second full term as president in 1968. It was a bumper year of public conflict asterisked by the deaths of Martin Luther King and Robert Kennedy and the riots in the ghetto streets of Newark, Los Angeles, Chicago, Atlanta, and Cleveland. That summer in Chicago at the Democratic National Convention, the Chicago police rioted, beating and terrorizing protestors and delegates alike on national network television.

Though the images of "war" in America were brought to the heartland and a street theater action was turned into nightly news broadcasts, in the long run it proved to be a gigantic miscalculation, since it gave authorities ample cause to employ their monopoly of force. But by then, the Movement was already imploding, rent apart by the conflicting political and social agendas that spilled chaotically onto the streets of Chicago and into Grant Park.

Though more people than ever demonstrated against the war and its ranks swelled in Chicago's aftermath, the mood of the demonstrations had shifted. Underneath now percolated a climate of random violence that wasn't there before, when the metaphor had been more pliant, general in its scope, and timeless in its appeal. Violence began to displace nonviolence as a general mode of action for the Movement. Peace became in a sense a finite commodity, meaning different things for different groups, a means to achieve individual agendas.

Sectarian factionalism dominated large organizational meetings where each group had its own unique agenda that had to be addressed. The war in Vietnam was really the war on poverty, racism, sexism of all kinds, persuasions, proclivities, a War of Liberation that was beginning to unfold in various forms in board rooms, offices, factories, classrooms, and courthouses throughout the land. For the far left it may have seemed to be "total assault on the culture," but no one any longer agreed on its tactics or its targets; we had met the enemy and it *was* us.[14] The Movement, a loose confederation of like-minded people at best, was atomized into its components, the varieties of socialism, communism (Russian, Chinese, and Cuban variations), and anarchism, civil rights and gender issues. There were Maoists, Trotskyites (who ran the office), and hardline Stalinists at odds with hardcore pacifists and gay rights activists. Everyone seemed to have his own shock troops in place to "liberate the community from the oppressor"—the full spectrum, from the Black Panthers, the extremist element of the civil rights movement, to the Hispanic Brown Berets to the WPP of Ann Arbor, Michigan, who believed in the power of sex, drugs, and rock and roll (preferably together) to knock it all loose. In New York City, even mental patients had their own Liberation League and storefront office.

Totally committed to violence was the Weather Underground, a group of the best and brightest, so elite one had to have a Triple-A Dun & Bradstreet rating to be a member (close, just kidding). Eventually they blew up their New York City townhouse/clubhouse with most of their leadership inside while assembling a home-made dynamite bomb. They were so far in the vanguard they never consulted anyone, preferring to issue press releases before and communiqués after the bombs went off. But their exception only proved the rule since everyone demanded his or her own unique piece of the action, while Whitman's idea of ensemble/individuality, which had somehow unified and energized the factions, was engulfed. Me, what about me?, they all cried.

But what had happened to *us?*

The Rolling Stones song "Street-Fighting Man," which in some small way had typified the protester's attitude in Chicago in 1968, by 1972 had in Miami Beach, Florida, been transformed. In Loomis Park (temporarily renamed People's Park for the duration) off Lower Collins Avenue, a staging area from which the Movement gathered in all its rainbow hues, one could now pick up at the green candy-striped party tent (more appropriate for a country club wedding) an official revolutionary songbook from Students for a Democratic Society (SDS). Progressive Labor Party organizers wore not Army surplus fatigues, but bright red T-shirts emblazoned with the slogan "Smash the State." Perhaps as an exercise in irony, they'd expropriated a popular soda commercial jingle to use in its war against America: "I'd like to teach the world to sing in perfect Mandarin/With Uncle Ho and Chairman Mao, Fidel and Madame Binh/Revolution, It's the Real Thing." *The Mickey Mouse Club* closing theme was no less usefully parodied; "Now it's time to say goodbye to all the bourgeoisie, etc." It wasn't ironic; it was pathetic and a little sad, too.

79

It was also here in front of this very same tent with these very same revolutionaries and the whole world watching (well it seemed to be, with so many cameras) that the late Allen Ginsberg, spiritual descendant of Walt Whitman, author of the Beat paean *Howl* and Movement peacecreep-in-residence, lost his temper when being told by the red shirts that "all art which doesn't serve the Revolution is counterproductive." In the same tones that he had chanted "AH" to any group or camera who would have him, he chanted "Fuck SDS, Fuck you, SDS, Fuck you, fuck you, fuck you" in anger and disgust. It was a shocking deviation from the script the organizers had put together, with even more disastrous results than 4 years before when chaos had reigned in the streets of Chicago.[15]

But in truth, it was only the media who cared now, for whose benefit the protests were staged, since for all intents and purposes the Movement had been overshadowed by the phenomenon known as the counterculture, whose attitudes and style an upcoming generation of youth inherited from their brothers and sisters, a club that included everyone under 30 whose distinguishing characteristics were a love and allegiance to sex, drugs, and rock and roll but that trivialized its import. No one really cared who Ho Chi Minh, Hermann Hesse, Samuel Beckett, Allan Watts, or even Walt Whitman was anymore, since no one seemed to have any more time to read at the big party, now that Nixon was withdrawing troops and the boys were coming home. Considering the forces that were and had been at work, it was inevitable that the music America listened to would be overwhelmed, drowning out the discourse that had been the cause of Whitman's essay *Democratic Vistas* almost a century earlier. Indeed, there was music in the air, mostly cash registers in this Brave New World, one that Walt Whitman had warily understood well enough from his nineteenth-century viewpoint, but would have disowned if alive then.

80   Question Authority? Whose? Not ours.

Shards

> It would be ironic if, at a time when many of the old institutions of adolescence are in manifest decline, spokesmen for the counterculture succeeded in creating a more sophisticated if no less pernicious version of adolescence, one that sanctions the isolation of youth from adult roles not because such roles "tempt" or "corrupt" the young but because they fail to provide scope for freedom and spontaneity.
>
> JOSEPH KETT[16]

> It just became something that was necessary. Really as a young person, it became socially necessary.
>
> KIP COHEN, manager of Fillmore East, on the counterculture[17]

By the summer of 1967, baptized forever after by the national news media as "The Summer of Love," the music of counterculture had already suffocated that feeling of ensemble/individuality that embodied both head culture and the coalition of forces represented by the anti-War movement. Growing in intensity for the previous year and a half, it had been primarily framed and publicized by the major media (newspapers, television, radio) with varying degrees of truth and insight as an urban or college town phenomenon. *Time, Life, Look, Newsweek, The Saturday Evening Post*—all supplied the colorful pictorials, analysis, and spin for everyone who lived outside the urban centers, where all "the action" was taking place.

Those urban and college enclaves were served by their own media, collectively known as the underground press, with all manner of alternative ideas on health and education, plus poetry and, of course, rock and roll concert and record reviews, the latter of which proved to be its undoing in the end. With varying degrees of effectiveness and candor, what came to be known as the underground press printed, unlike some of their establishment colleagues, not only all the news that was fit to sing about the War but all related activities: protests, vigils, etc. New York City had the *East Village Other* and *Rat;* Boston, *The Phoenix;* Los Angeles, the *LA Free Press;* San Francisco, *The Oracle,* as the *Berkeley Barb* and *Bay Area Guardian.* There were papers as well in Austin, Texas, Atlanta, Georgia, and all points in between.

While counterculture was being brokered to the youth under 30, as a "lifestyle" engendered by the sacred triad of sex, drugs, and rock and roll, the historical, literate, and timeless concepts that formerly underpinned it all (as well as the indigenous folk origins of the music) were unceremoniously jettisoned, substituted by the vagaries of a fashion-mediated peer group pressure tactically exploited by various interested parties, especially (but not limited to) the music business. Floundering in the early sixties, it had been revivified by the popularity of folk rock and the English pop invasion of the Beatles, the

Stones. and others. as well as the sounds of psychedelia emanating from San Francisco and Los Angeles. It was here that the
so-called counterculture made its most visible economic effect.
so that by the late sixties there was no record company worth its
name that didn't have on its payroll at least a few long-haired
"company freaks," former political activists or underground
music journalists involved in the various aspects and mechanics
of the business, from advertising to promotion to the development of new artists and repertoire.

By 1968 rock and revolution had become inextricably linked
in the public mind, or at least with the record-buying public
mind, as a youth fashion statement, which came to be typified by
a Columbia Records ad campaign designed by Jim Fouratt. A
former actor and social activist in San Francisco's Haight Ash-
bury in the midsixties as well as an associate of Dr. Timothy Leary,
Fouratt conceived of a print ad campaign that prominently featured a picture of a group of hippies in a jail holding pen under
the tag line,"The Man Can't Bust Our Music." Cool, huh?

There was some kind of logic to all of this: the media
freaks, a new elite, working on the inside of multimillion-dollar
corporations to subvert corporate America and effect cultural
change. Though at the time it seemed like an ideal gig with free
typewriters, phones, mail, photocopying, and associated promotional goodies and etceteras, one had to walk a fine line to justify
having all those perks and to maintain one's credibility—if only
to oneself. Anyway, it was only a matter of time before one
would have to work on something that really sucked but that the
company had spent a pile on, when the "revolutionary" agent in
place on the inside teetered on the edge or fell off. Some did,
some didn't, but it was fun while it lasted—a hell of an education in the ways of the world for those who tried to serve two
masters and then found that they were serving only Mammon.

If one views the music business of that time as a full field
metaphor for how contemporary cultural ideas were transacted,

brokered, and subtly (or not so subtly) changed by the commercial environment, it's easier to understand the mechanism by which the loosely defined head culture became the visibly fashionable counterculture, which in turn led to the "Me Generation" disco-quaalude shuffle of the seventies and its punk antithesis, to the cocaine-fueled "yuppie" vogueing of the eighties, and eventually to the jacked-in hip-hop information superhighway boogie of the nineties.

More to the point, the commodification process has informed and driven American cultural life since the middle of the nineteenth century, of which the McLuhanesque sixties electric/psychedelic variant was the result. It's what William Leach, in *Land of Desire*, a cultural history of department stores and their merchandizing techniques, characterized as "the cult of the new," which "readily subverted whatever custom, value, or folk idea came within its reach."[18] In essence this happened when head culture was commercially reinvented and brokered as counterculture a process that continues unabated and is rarely commented upon today. To Jim Morrison of the Doors, music may have been your only friend until the end in the late sixties, but there was all that time before the Apocalypse that had to be filled with "product." It was here the underground press and the culture it was to represent in some small way went adrift and aground.

83

In the beginning, it made good business sense. In exchange for record company support through full-, half-, or quarter-page ads, underground newspaper publishers were able to upgrade and expand the coverage of peace-related events, while the critics' low-paying wages were effectively subsidized by free records, concert tickets, and club tabs. This in turn fed the record business merchandizing machine. (They would have done it in any case without the other perks, but the perks helped.) Living in a state of cultural fast-forward, months ahead of the wave and surfeited with all kinds of "inside information," the critics themselves became estranged from their own audience. The more they became an integral part of the brokerage business, the more cynical they became about their audience. And instead of being content to be merely reporters, they became active players in the commercial dance themselves, using their position to search out newer and newer trends to exploit for their own critical self-aggrandizement, to become celebrities themselves within an increasingly celebrity-driven subculture.

When the music was transcendent and vital, rock critics in the underground press easily maintained their integrity and wrote inspiring prose; but when the music was not so good, or egregiously awful, it was a harder job, because the record companies still expected—nay, demanded—uncritical support in exchange for their advertising revenues. Publishers as best as they could tried to explain the situation with varying degrees of success. Though this unstated quid pro quo between publisher and advertiser may have been an old dance for the establishment media book, movie, and music critics from time immemorial (as is currently unofficially practiced by major newspapers of record), it was a shocking wake-up call to these new kids who thought everyone ought to play by their rules. Some papers who tried to buck the system folded because they lost their financial base, while others—like *Rolling Stone*, which had other sources of revenue and a solid demographic base—hung tough until the record companies themselves backed down and some kind of modus vivendi was negotiated. Some critics joined record companies, others quit to be replaced by more pliant, less fastidious souls who were in it for the perks just like any other art-promotion job. Though it may not have been a pretty sight, it was the way of the world, then as now.

All was made immeasurably easier by Nixon's strategy of gradually ending the War, which removed the underground press's political and social vitality, substituting for it issues of style—hence the birth of the disgusting term "lifestyle"—which were all that remained. In a few short years, the protest of the

American Way, which was running amok in Southeast Asia and throughout the world, had ironically (to the old heads) become a *commercial* celebration. One 4-year high school generation's introspection and soul-searching became an entitlement, the right to party for the next's.

By the summer of 1969 there was a certain desperate quality to it that Patricia Kennealy Morrison, editor of *Jazz and Pop* magazine, noted at the Woodstock Music and Art Fair ("Three Days of Peace and Music"). Amid the good times she saw ominous signs at the birth of the "Woodstock Nation" that both establishment and counterculture media, in its sanctification of the event, chose to overlook:

> Yes, the kids are beautiful; yes I *was* Out There with them, and I did see a great deal of beauty. But also I saw thousands upon thousands of walking wounded of this Revolution we all talk so much about; kids who hadn't got faces yet, filled up with drugs they don't know how to make proper use of and only take because the Scene makes it easy. Kids like that hurt me; I feel media guilt, that maybe we who are older and supposed to know better did this to them (they're turning on in elementary schools now . . .) before they were ready for it; the kids that try to hitch a ride on your car with a V-sign, then snarl viciousness at you when you tiredly explain you have a full car and can't take any more passengers, the kids who have all the right hip clothes and know all the right words and drop all the right stuff but whose *heads* haven't been affected in the slightest; the kids who have come to this festival and are going to consume vibes and dope and music but what are they going to take home with them? Just as importantly, what have they brought?[19]

85

And what do they bring today?

The Era of Peace and Love had a short shelf-life indeed, lasting less than 6 months before its antithesis, the antifestival at Altamont, took place. Here, Hell's Angels who'd been hired as security guards for a free concert featuring the Rolling Stones, Grateful Dead, Jefferson Airplane, and others stabbed to death a concertgoer in front of tens of thousands of people.[20] To Kip

Cohen, the manager of New York's Fillmore East, a premier
East Coast mecca for rock and roll, the Woodstock generation
appeared to be nothing more than an aggressive gluttonous audience whose members were far more concerned about how
they looked than who they came to hear, whose tastes could be
extrapolated from the detritus left at 4 AM for the clean-up
crew—Romilar bottles and Trojans under the seats.[21]

Back to business as usual: New audiences demanded
newer music, newer trends; paisley prints, granny glasses, and
grass gave way to glitter, platform shoes, and speed soon
enough. The late sixties saw the emergence of heavy metal
music, which, though popular among the adolescent crowd,
was in reality hype-driven, showy, and musically bankrupt save
as pop sociology—which is how some rock critics framed coverage of the shows when they themselves could no longer deal
with these new audiences or their music. Groups like Grand
Funk Railroad and Black Sabbath were becoming the rage with
younger audiences just coming into their majority.

Those groups gave their audience the vulgarity they demanded. According to Kip Cohen, "everything the audience
wants, which is loudness, rudeness, lack of originality."[22] How
now? If the members of the underground press wished to retain
their authority as viable spokesmen for the culture they were
supposed to represent, they had to shift their focus away from
the politics of liberation (boring and beside the point to this
demanding adolescent world) toward the politics of cultural
consumption which was how the Establishment media had promoted and framed head culture to begin with.

Unlike head culture, which attempted to "do away" with
goods of all sorts by eschewing the heedless consumption of the
American way of life, counterculture reveled in it and was
served by an alternative though equally rapacious infrastructure
of long-haired dope-smoking retailers, merchandisers, and brokers of "hip capitalism" to service the adolescent needs for play

equipment, which the underground press uncovered and exploited. Johan Huizinga in 1936 caught an earlier part of this wave when he observed in his book *In the Shadow of History* that the play attitude of adolescents even then had become a permanent feature of Western culture whose emergence was "facilitated not only by a decreased desire for individual judgement, by the standardizing effect of group organizations providing a set of ready-made opinions, but also by the marvelous development of technical facilities."[23] And that's what electronically altered teenage money did with the sixties in the end.

Indeed, the real import of the sixties was *not* the making of the counterculture, but the selling of it, whereby the concept of Whitman's individuality/ensemble became translated and reduced to terms of "lifestyle choice," with the result that the nineties seems to be composed of a vast sea of passive spectator consumers awash in individuated goods that though insidiously varied, have little real value, a situation that has proved to be spiritually enervating to all who have been touched by it, and that's everyone who's alive now. In the process of blaming the sixties we are blaming ourselves for having lost the vision of America, which, however brief and fragile and imperfect, was nevertheless empowering and transcendent for all. Those who blame the sixties now are distraught and angry, and because the vision of the GE All-Electric Kitchen that Ronald Reagan sold on *Death Valley Days* not only came with a hefty price tag, but didn't (or never did) work—and we're stuck with it anyway. It's easy to blame the sixties rather than try to correct the commercial excesses that continue to inform every aspect of our lives. Blaming won't make the corruption go away; blame just amplifies and highlights its truth.

Now that nostalgia is driving history's engine, it's convenient for the left and the right to manipulate times past to their own ends since they can assume no one remembers. They think that images and slogans will suffice because they think they control the imagery now. Blame it on the sixties? The sixties blames

them for believing in the lie they collaborated upon, for de-
luding themselves, for believing in the goodness of goods instead of asking something of the humans who make them.

The sixties in its purest form was a shining historical moment that was supposed to raise consciousness, not deaden it,
to focus attention then broaden it from the singular to the universal. It was not meant to be brokered by goods, fashion, or
style, which weakened its total effect. It was never supposed to
be enumerated by statistical polls of ever-narrowing focus
groups and in fact lost its power when it was reduced in such a
manner. The sixties was about the freedom to question and arrive at answers and still question more, because The Way was
not simply the destination. Only in a closed and dead universe
were there invariable and inviolate answers. The true spirit of
the sixties, not counterculture or its subsequent peregrinations
and material permutations, believed in nonrepresentational
living, free of endorsement contracts, where one didn't have to
be true to one's high school alma mater.

Blame it on the the sixties? Well, the "sixties" blames the
left and the right for misapprehending its brief moment of
truth, for confusing and then preferring style over substance,
and for ultimately evading the questions our children pose
when we aren't "us" around them now that they want to know
all about it. Bring back the sixties? They haven't gone anywhere.
If we no longer can or want to remember those old sorehead
democratic vistas we saw for America in the sixties, the kids can
start with Walt Whitman. You never know; they could be inspired by him, too.

Chapter 4

Boxers or Briefs?
Music Politics in the Post-Elvis Age

For every jump-suited popstar sipping piña coladas by pools, there are thousands of guys strung out along the of nameless small town desolations getting nickled and dimed to death. Roll *that* up and smoke it.

RODRIGUEZ.[1]

It was during the 1992 presidential election on MTV's Town Meeting that the "depth" of the interpenetration between the rock and roll world and politics was reached, when candidate Bill Clinton was asked *that* deadly question: Boxers or briefs, which underwear style did he prefer? Constituencies must be solicited and candidates endure all manner of ritual indignities and abuse from the voters every 4 years, true, but what struck me most was not so much the question's insipid cuteness or the feeble attempt at "cutting-edge" humor—true irony requires an exact sense of history to give it some nuanced weight. Was this query supposed to elicit a knowing nod from generational coreligionists at home: "Hi, look at me, ain't I cool on MTV?" Though for me it sort of lay out there in electronic space like soggy cereal, this smartass question produced a ripple of nervous titters from the studio audience that night, and for days thereafter in the popular press.

Big deal, so the question was a slogan lifted from a popular Hanes advertising campaign. But I was puzzled. Was the question more on the lines of "How do you see yourself under your suit of clothes, the suit of clothes we all perforce must wear in our daily lives?" or "What image are you trying to promote with your underwear?" or "What's the first metaphor you put on in the morning to cover yourself?" Is underwear and not what's under the wear the true measure of a politician's inner soul? Are presidents really elected on the basis of a nuanced understanding of an advertising campaign that turns underwear into an item of competition and style, or does this sort of advertising only have resonance for MTV's target audience? Was this the political face of official music culture now: boxers or briefs?

91

Were Bush and Clinton supposed to frame their whole debate and discussion of America's future within the parameters
of adspeak, which would be framed in the postmortem media
wrap-ups as "Taste Great. Less Filling. Voters choose?" That's a
far more accurate assessment of the level of understanding and
discernment the major political parties expect from the national
electorate every few years. What would have happened if the
candidates had been hip enough to reply "none of the above,"
neatly blind-siding the smug little twerp and forcing him to
think about other realities besides the brand name one he was
contemplating and inhabiting? "That's all you can come up
with?" replies the candidate with a twinkle in his eye. When did
one's choice in underwear become the be-all and end-all of political wisdom? Maybe I was just thinking too hard; but given the
chance, what sort of question would youth have asked 25 years
ago when the only forums that belonged to the people were the
streets? Times have changed. Stop the sketch.

This all was too "out" to contemplate until I remembered
that this debate was sponsored by the *news* division of MTV.
What *news?* MTV news consists of equal parts of record company promo hype, rock celebrity gossip, and tidbits about
what's in and out in the music world—it's just another network
like ABC, NBC, CBS, or Fox. From its humble beginnings as a
depository for record company promotional videos, in a little
more than a decade MTV now produces sitcoms, game shows,
special features, and phony self-promoting award shows. Like its
older siblings, MTV also works on cultivating and refining its audience demographics to increase its advertising revenues with
commercials for beer, cars, and blemish cream for the Lite beer
set. In going for the gold, MTV has much abused the "spirit of
rock and roll," especially if they mean the feeling of the pure joy
of being that rock and roll music unlocks which has little to do
with the "goodness of the goods": the ownership of cars, lipstick, or credit cards. MTV's just like *Rolling Stone* magazine, its
print equivalent, which started off "alternative and outlaw" and
gnarly 'round the edges in the late sixties, which now rivals *Es-*

quire and the *New Yorker* in terms of total feel (if not in content) and in terms of the number of full-color ads for major brand-name merchandise. Since it has become part of the Viacom Communications conglomerate, MTV has had even less to do with music or the spirit of rock and roll and has become more involved in the business until it now basically functions as a junior media executive farm team for the Bigs.

"The spirit of Rock and Roll"—I like that.

What if the MTV Town Meeting audience, instead of being demographically correct, was comprised of people who liked rock and roll in all its forms, commercial and uncommercial; if instead of wiseacres whose brains had been permanently damaged by advertising the audience was composed of real fans well into it—heavy metal fans and hip-hoppers, rude-boys and gang-bangers with a dash of suburban snotnoses—to whom the candidates would have had to exhibit their intergenerational knowledge of musically nuanced behavior. One hell of a test for the MTV demographic, eh?

93

What if a fanatic biker messenger/bungee jumper with a orange mohawk asked a question on foreign policy which lit-reffed Henry Kissinger or better Otto von Bismarck on the value of *realpolitik?* Would Bill Clinton have charmingly let slip to some earnest prog-rocker that at Yale law school he was such a big Mothers of Invention/Zappa freak that he had a Phi Krappa Zappa poster on his dorm room wall, or that his wife-to-be ripped it off the wall during a spat, or that when he went to visit President Vaclav Havel of the Czech Republic he brought him a stack of Zappa CDs? What would the voters hypothetically have made of a revelation from either candidate who admitted to a serious jones for Nine Inch Nails, NWA, or ZZ Top, or was an un-regenerate C&W fanatic (well, hell, everyone has a soft spot for C&W)? It would be informative to voters to learn just what part music played in the soundtrack of their lives. Had rap lyrics gone too far? Why? Youth wants to know. Answers to these questions

would have shown that Bill and George were at least human,
provided their answers were honest sound bite McNuggets.

Dream on, Walley. The context would have been lost on the
MTV crowd the candidates were working that night, consumers
for whom reality is nice concept so long as it's correctly packaged. Preposterous? Absolutely. It wasn't a political debate that
was going on here anyway, but rather a canny business decision
that exploited the division between the generations in which the
MTV corporate ethos so heavily invests. Let's face it, the only
people who have no stake at all in resolving the conflict between
the generations are the advertisers and the fabricators of generational goods who have the most to lose. It wouldn't do on other
levels because MTV understands that most young people (adolescents to early 30s these days) are heavily invested in the fiction
that somehow politicians and/or celebrities are not real human
beings. It's one thing to know friends of your parents who are
cool, and quite another for your parents themselves to be cool
and be forced to acknowledge it because, by definition, parents
aren't cool. It goes against the creed that only youth are entitled
to have any kind of inner life of which music is a vital part. That
also wouldn't reveal an admittedly informed understanding of
"the enemy" in the either/or, black/white world of the ever-
changing *now*, not one bit. Boxers are Briefed?

If MTV *really* embodied the real spirit of rock and roll,
they could have dispensed with the Town Meeting entirely, and
instead featured a Battle of the Bands with Lee Atwater, George
Bush's late campaign manager and a self-styled blues guitar
strangler, playing against Clinton staff wanna-be irregulars.
Bottom line, whoever put together the most ass-kicking, heart-
stopping set of rock and roll would have been declared the
winner. And if there had to be candidates at all, have them
sucking on humongous bongs while seated at a back table at
House of Blues or Hard Rock Cafe, critiquing the set or dis-
cussing the nature of the interface between politics and music.
Awesome, dude. Twenty-five years ago, heads weren't so totally

befuddled by the celebrity of politicians (or the celebrity of themselves for that matter) *not* to ask why we were in Vietnam. In that more naive age, young people were less accepting of corporate culture and wisdom, if only because when the rhetoric of patriotism was stripped away from the Vietnam War, they understood just how it was used to defend the rights of corporate interests to exploit Southeast Asia's natural resources, just like France and Japan had failed to do. So much for neat metaphors. Indeed, it is paradoxical that in the nineties, the spirit of rock and roll that spoke to the best of a generation's aspirations has become a hostage to a corporate culture whose implicit assumptions are just as invidious as the ones that generation attempted with varying degrees of success to overcome, replace, or at least humanize. These days those connections are harder to pinpoint, hidden as they are within an innerconnected lattice of special interest posturings, PR releases, and media conglomerates.

But what would have happened if instead of employing a cute political affairs celebrity-journalist like Tabatha Soren, MTV brought in Hunter S. Thompson as moderator? Father of Gonzo journalism and author of *Fear and Loathing on the Campaign Trail*, Thompson wrote the archetypal new journalism *ur*-text of drug-tinged political paranoia in the 1972 presidential campaign. Bet that George Bush wouldn't have been as threatened as Saxophone Bill (for whom Hunter Thompson's attitude at one time had a deep generational resonance, maybe more than he'd care to admit in public now). Provided the good doctor was more or less "behaving" himself (however he defined "behavior" and the management agreed), an instructive though dangerous vision would have resulted, raising the level of political discourse a few notches—if the intent of the exercise was to bring rock and rollers of all ages together instead of merely the MTV demographic. In truth, that spectacle would have been too visually ragged to be used for pitching big ticket commercial accounts, which in management's point of view was the ultimate point of the exercise. The rest of us would hope that, true to form, Dr. Thompson would rip through the proceedings like the psychic bull in a china shop we think he'd be and not give a rat's ass whether he looked good on camera on not. *This* would not do at all, nor would it be true to the nature of political discourse in the Post-Elvis Age.

Talk about the devolution of political discourse! Whole universes and countless light-years separate the writing style and mind-set of Hunter Thompson from our own. Our politicians today don't even merit paranoid fear and loathing—instead we treat them like any other contemporary whose opinion we don't like: We flat out disrespect them, to hell with the reasons why. Instead of Thompson's darkly twisted and richly multileveled surrealist universe, the political pundits of left and right have relocated to the parking lot before school or the locker-lined high school hallway. There, while changing classes, they rank on each other: "Hey asshole." "No, you're an asshole." "And you're a fuckhead." "That's *Mister* Fuckhead to you," etc. Is it any wonder that comedian Al Franken's collection of political essays, *Rush Limbaugh Is a Big Fat Idiot,* has been a recent bestseller in this bravest of new worlds where attitude is the only thing? Breathlessly one awaits his sequel, *Newt Gingrich Is a Big Fat Idiot Too.* Dude, go for it!!

Not to be outdone, the neoconservatives weigh in with their own heavy hitters, represented by a Rush Limbaugh or a P. J. O'Rourke, who view national and international affairs from the comparatively "enlightened" perspective of a beer-besotted fratrat or know-it-all high school cadet who, joint in hand, from his perch on the sink in the Boys Room, disparages the efforts of the spirit committee (do-gooding, soft-minded liberal Democrats, aging peaceniks and their [ahem] weak-kneed wussy New Age-demented neohippie ecologist spawn) in their efforts to clean up the karma at Screaming Eagle High. A far more formally critical though similar discourse style defines as it distinguishes *The New Republic* from R. Emmett Tyrell's *American Spectator,* or even the editorial overview of *The Wall Street*

Journal from *The New York Times*. Which is puzzling because Franken, O'Rourke, and many contemporary commentators on American culture have been exposed to, if they haven't actually been beneficiaries of, Thompson's ground-breaking journalistic methodology and attitude. Instead of using it as a staging area from which to launch more pertinent public forms of political analysis and discourse, in their hands it becomes a tool for finagling power-politics dinner party invitations; in effect, to better buy into the world Thompson illuminated while simultaneously undermining its base assumptions. For the new bosses (who are the same as the old bosses), things are just fine, because the spoils of the game as they've defined it, celebrity and insider status, are far easier to deal with than the responsibilities they'd have moderating a dialogue in which everyone else is included. And while these BMOCs are inside collaborating with the principal, so to speak, we're left loitering in another smelly high school corridor . . . again. Celebrity consumerhood makes for stranger bedfellows in the Post-Elvis Age.

Boxers or briefs? It really doesn't make much of a difference to MTV's mindset—they reason it's "our" corporate culture, rock and roll's, or better, MTV's vision of the rock and roll world, as opposed to "theirs" (ConGlomCo Inc.'s). Or so they've successfully deluded themselves into thinking. Long ago it possibly may have been true that "The Man Can't Bust Our Music," but there's no reason why the corporate "we" of MTV can't spin control and homogenize the spirit if not the effect of rock and roll. No matter how revolutionary, apposite, faintly or potentially seditious to the survival the music might be, eventually it becomes just another transitory celebrity product and lifestyle statement. And like other entertainment media, MTV dispenses the myth that with "access," everyone can be an "insider"—the highest social benefit this celebrity-driven society confers. To be an insider, all one has to do is follow the rules of deportment as codified by MTV personalities, just like high school all over again, or the audiovisual equivalent; everyone watches TV. Within this smug all-access-backstage-pass world of celebrity maps, MTV supplies to its consumers a carbon copy of the Hollywood movie version of celebrity. When the media spotlight shines out, we all know what to expect and what is expected from us. Access also peddles supermarket tabloids like *The Star* or *The Globe*, the "news/gossip" programs on E! (Entertainment Channel), *Entertainment Tonight*, and CNN, or tabloid TV like *Hard Copy*, *20/20*, *Dateline*, and even *60 Minutes*. MTV's continued success both here and abroad is a testament to just how right they've been in handicapping the trends of youth. Though far removed from the original "spirit of rock and roll," judging from how rapidly the company has been absorbed into the larger corporate media maw of ConGlomCo Entertainments, Inc., it's been a good business decision nonetheless.

If all we're really talking about is consumer choice, the connection between rock music and politics used to be easier to make; perhaps our definition of goods has been altered over the past quarter century. It could be safely, if generally, assumed 25 years ago that on some level the kind of politics rock and roll audiences responded to hinged on a belief in the political and moral ramifications of understanding, equality, cooperation, and unity wrapped around a beat that was also great to boogie to. In 1971 that mind-set inspired George Harrison, Bob Dylan, and Eric Clapton, along with other rock superstars, to sponsor the Concert for Bangladesh, a benefit concert with a subsequent record album merchandising tie-in that raised more than $300,000 for Bangladeshi flood relief. The events set the media formula and standard that paved the way for international music fundraisers like Live Aid, the Mandala Tributes, Amnesty International's Conspiracy of Hope and Human Rights, and, in the United States, the No-Nukes concerts and Farm Aid benefits, all of which have raised tens of millions of dollars for charity, making rock music fund-raisers a common fixture on the cultural landscape.

Though the publicity build-ups, the good will, and/or cash raised have been awesome, afterwards there always seems to be a dearth of follow-up stories concerning the percentage of total monies that were finally dispersed to the causes. Unfortunately, most people tend to ignore the economics of charity benefits. Celebrities may donate their time, but rarely do they forego the limo to and from the gig or, if from out of town, the plane tickets and associated hotel rooms that come with the package. Even if performance fees are donated or waived, the care and feeding of the rest of the concert support team—stagehands, electricians, video, satellite, and sound technicians/directors— also cost somebody in the end. Feeling good having donated some money to the cause, people move on, and the connection is reinforced that cash donations are a covalent substitute for real-time social commitment—no foul, no blame.

With benefits cropping up seemingly every 3 months, though, once we are habituated to the event structure and the proper response to it, these events start losing their emotional punch and political significance because in the broadest terms, one "good" cause is much like another. Okay, so people are dying somewhere, goes the interior monologue, they're starving in droves, their ecology is in the toilet because of clear-cutting, and they're oppressed as shit, okay, that sucks, here's my money to help fix it, now let's get down and boogie. In a nanosecond, the political cause becomes a petty annoyance. Ignoring the scrolling messages at the bottom of the TV set listing the 1-800 donation numbers, we intently concentrate on the depoliticized entertainment event, the ever-changing mini-drama/soap opera of music business politics in which everyone is alleged to be an insider, as familiar a world to us as watching the Oscars now that Whoopi Goldberg, Billy Crystal, or Robin Williams are the emcees. Once that donation for the T-shirt/CD package is American Expressed, Master-, or Visa-carded, we shift our attention to who shows up, how they look, and who's backing up whom. There are all kinds of musicians: those who are there just because they like to jam and party, but not exclusive to Rod Stewart, as well as those, like certain Hollywood celebrities, whose media political commitment is exquisitely of the moment, who mastered the delicate knack for being associated with each and every newsworthy cause du jour. It takes a while to figure out who they are.

We psych ourselves up for that quintessential musical/historical "moment" every benefit claims it will produce. Perhaps there will be a "reunion" of an old classic rock band who've gone their separate ways, but, swallowing their egos and their pride, reunite for One Night Only to play the good old stuff (largely left until that closing jam session). "Reunions" of Cream, Led Zeppelin, or The Who are way up there near the top of that event structure possibility. (And wouldn't it be cool if some rock and roll New Age psychic guitarist channeled Kurt Cobain back from his final reward and the donations skyrocketed, proving the economic clout—or political commitment— of grunge-rockers to the old hippies who continue to organize these shows?) If not whole bands reunited, then it's an elevating thing to witness the resurrection of a supposed "has-been" or enjoy the appearance of a "mystery" celebrity guaranteed to burn down the house and take no prisoners—Little Richard, Chuck Berry, Jerry Lee Lewis, or Bob Dylan can't do that enough. Whether some careers are resurrected or spectacularly crash and burn makes for riveting media politics worthy of the combo donation for the T-shirt/CD/tape. Truth is, some shows raise more money than others and are as much dependent on the political (or celebrity) correctness of the cause as the number or the celebrity of the musicians involved.

Though we might prefer to think otherwise, pop music is politically neutral, its fund/political consciousness-raising capabilities are not the exclusive property of liberal, socialist, or environmentalist agendas. There are as many if no less prominent (and not-so-prominent) pop musicians who support the political right and the Religious Right. Though not as well-publicized, pop, rock, and country music artists also raise funds for and/or the spirits of neo-Nazi skinheads, survivalists, segregationists, and right-to-life advocates just as handily. So do evangelical Christians in their parallel pop worlds, who have not only their own rappers and heavy metal gospel maniacs but also a whole supporting universe that music unlocks with its own cable networks, magazines, and fan support groups. And please do not forget the enduring presence within the past 25 years of certain forms of heavy metal music whose adherents give their allegiance (symbolically or actually) to His Satanic Majesty, Old Scratch. As far as this writer knows, however, Lucifer doesn't resort to rock benefits to raise money, much as the Religious Right would like to think; the devil has been around longer than consumerist capitalism.

In the main, rock and roll has been apolitical, a public-access folk medium through which many ideas can be funneled and electrically transmuted, a medium that takes on the protective coloration of anyone happens to be using it—with some notable exceptions. In the mideighties the Reagan Administration theoretically could have staged a series of rock and roll benefits for Contra Aid, though one wonders who would have shown up (as well as who would have said what in the media about whom). I suspect that's because many musicians are either apolitical or liberal, if only because the nature of their work environment encourages them to be so, thus creating a patently absurd, almost virtually unthinkable scenario. So depending on how one looks at it, it was either lucky or very unlucky in terms of the subsequent Iran-Contra hearings that Ronald Reagan's advisors chose to draw financial support from other sources with far deeper pockets than the audience for pop music whose good will, since his days as the governor of California in the seventies, he had never been interested in cultivating in the first place. And playing Jimi Hendrix on his press plane during the 1992 election didn't help Dan Quayle prove to the pool reporters that he was one of the guys and a card-carrying rock and roll fiend either. Even when the fact was generally known, it didn't raise anybody's consciousness very much—especially his.

Boxers in Briefs: A Vogue Pictorial?

The term "erotic politician," which in the sixties was used to describe the ability of a Jim Morrison, Jimi Hendrix, or John Lennon to fuse together sexuality with populist politics (the term was, in fact, coined by Morrison, no mean manipulator himself; the media pounced on it, as of course he had coolly and deliberately intended them to), in the nineties now extends to music personalities like Madonna, Ru Paul, or The Artist Formerly Known as Prince (TAFKAP for short). Their influence is more evident in the style section of major metropolitan dailies or on the pages of *Vogue*, *Rolling Stone*, or *Spin* magazines than on the street, which, or so it once was said, belonged to the people (maybe the Internet is its equivalent these days).

Unfortunately, when the impetus for change has come from the streets, as in the case of hip-hop and rap, whatever power that music possessed has been inevitably homogenized, rapidly accessorized, and turned into a commodity by the official style council media in its over-the-counter configuration. With so much information and so little time to digest it all, it's far easier to reduce everything to the gestural shorthand of "lifestyle," politics included. We no longer "live our lives" as much as partake of a certain "lifestyle" that, according to advertising motivational researchers and political pollsters, is supposed to represent who we are and what we believe, which they extrapolate from the quantity and quality of the things we consume. When political ideology is viewed in terms of a lifestyle choice, personal commitments are transitory, easily made and just as easily broken and involving about as much effort as it takes to switch from a Big Mac to a Whopper or to choose a different or more effective antidepressant medication (well, this *is* the nineties). The consequences that result from framing political ideology in terms of competing lifestyle choices may seem negligible, but only because the style councils provide us with a shallow, misinformed sense of what this means for us in the longer run.

There's no reason why wanna-be singer/songwriter-turned-mass-murder Charlie Manson shouldn't be added to our short list of erotic politicians along with Michael Jackson and Madonna. Charlie most certainly had an effect on the generation of the sixties with his attempt to use rock's persuasive powers to promote political change, and wasn't he successful (on a microlevel, surely) in selling his followers the concept of the Beatles' *White Album* as apocalyptic text? And speaking of Apocalypse, why not include David Koresh as well? Before founding the Branch Davidian sect, which in a fiery shootout with federal authorities spectacularly self-destructed on nation-wide TV, Koresh as lead guitarist fronted a merry band of apocalyptic fundamentalist Christians, whose aim was to harness the power of the gospels for what he thought was the good of humankind. Koresh was not unlike John Lennon in that regard, save that Lennon used an alternative set of gospels for an entirely different end. Deluded and self-destructive though Koresh or Manson may have been to their followers and themselves, their use of music shows how powerful an intellectual intoxicant pop music can be as a force for political change whether we choose to acknowledge the veracity of the politics they promote or not.

Though not of the *Vogue* mold (though you never know when their fashion *zeitgeist* will come back as a runway "lifestyle") and to Koresh's and Manson's dubious credit, as disturbed as they were, at least these two decidedly alternative erotic politicians had pretensions to be cultural revolutionaries, not fashion plates or strategists attached to the vanguard of the cultural revolution as the major media style councils see and promote themselves. Music is primarily fashion-driven these days, they assume; when we buy the music of Madonna, Michael Jackson, or David Bowie, or follow the leads of quasi-music personalities like Dennis Rodman (the cross-dressing pro basketball player and sometime MTV personality), instead of being passive consumers we are active supporters of the cultural revolution whose inside track they alone are privy to.

They've almost convinced us that these artists—along with socialites, supermodels, clothing designers, and glitterati of the
moment who are also part of the pop music world—are really
sixties-style cultural revolutionaries in disguise, and, at the risk
of being shunned as unmutual, uncool, or backward-looking
deluded socialist soreheads, we may as well just bend over and
enjoy it.

They're wrong, of course, and it just shows to go you how
language has also become a function of entertainment culture
over the past 25 years. According to Robert G. Pielke's in-
sightful and cogently argued study of rock and roll music, *You
Say You Want a Revolution: Rock Music in American Culture*,
cultural revolutions have six major characteristics: (1) they embody a fundamental challenge to prevailing values; (2) they are
never rapid; (3) they produce strong counterreactions; (4) they
are not merely political; (5) they are not intrinsically violent;
and (6) they tend toward the expansion of individual freedom.[2]
By these criteria, few if any of today's style council "cultural
revolutionaries" would measure up. It might no longer seem to
matter what happens to today's cultural revolutionaries who
do.

When politics and music converge in the rock music benefit context, music business politics always leads. For artists, it
makes good business sense, since appearing at a high-profile
benefit has just as much commercial and career-making potential as having a chart-topping hit—only without the needless ex-
pense (or headache) of mounting an expensive promotional
tour. For stars between album releases, a judicious benefit appearance is a prime venue in which to premiere new material
for a live CD-buying or concert-going audience. Record companies and their executives are equally well served by this system.
For the comparatively minimal cost of underwriting a benefit's
expenses, they gain the intangible corporate asset of "goodwill,"
if not for themselves personally, then for the companies they
represent, for "bragging rights" if you will.

And here's how it works: The higher profile the cause, the bigger the media hype with a larger audience of potential consumers accruing from the hype and the more potential and eventual consumer interest in new material. However, even a good thing can be taken to extremes in the protean world of rock and roll politics, because exclusive and full-time political commitments can be guaranteed instant career killers once the cause is out of the public eye and ear. This maxim is generally true save for superstars like Bruce Springsteen, Bob Dylan, and a few others whose careers and reputations are secure. Having made more than enough money, and if only as a form of psychic payback, these stars have the leisure to do "the good work" whether it is au courant or not. And thank God they can and do, because contrary to popular belief, record companies cannot and will not make those statements.

105

Call it the worship of the bottom line, or simply naked self-interest, but from a record company's point of view not all causes are equal, nor are all fights "good." From the public relations standpoint, Blitzbomp Records (not its real name), a large multinational entertainment conglomerate, may feel all warm and fuzzy supporting famine relief, or say, a flashy celebrity-studded benefit for PEN, the international writer's organization that pressures foreign governments to stop censoring and imprisoning politically inconvenient writers, because, objectively, the cause is politically neutral. On the other hand, Blitzbomp will *not* be so moved to support any benefit that informs the public about its own artistic censorship or economic exploitation, which routinely takes place within their own company or the record industry as a whole; it's simply too close to home, simply not done, everybody knows. Grin and bear it. Indeed, it is a system every bit as totalitarian and repressive as any Eastern European or South American dictatorship that keeps artists, save for the very rich and famous, in perpetual slavery. These are the true politics of the music business and the business of music, and it goes like this:

How the Kleptos Lost Their Boxers: A Cautionary Table

The Kleptos (not their real name) sign with Blitzbomp Records, a subsidiary of ConGlomCo Entertainment (a.k.a The Company) for $500,000. Though this might seem like a small fortune for the band, who have been scuffling for years, it's chump change, since The Company also signed three other bands for a comparable sum. If one band makes it, Blitzbomp—having played the law of averages—is still ahead of the curve. In exchange for this advance against future royalties, the band obligates itself to produce two albums with an option for a third. In effect, the group is leasing their artistic product, the master recordings, to Blitzbomp, who will distribute the product to record outlets far and wide. Only after The Company deducts its operating costs (manufacturing, distribution, promotion) and the standard prearranged percentage and pays the songwriting royalties and mechanicals will the band start making money, or so it is assumed.

Sounds good enough, think our boys, who commence acting like the rock and roll warriors they always wanted to be. Immediately, they upgrade their equipment, perhaps invest in a new PA system for the road or trade in the van for a good used touring bus. The lead guitarist drops his current girlfriend for an up-and-coming supermodel, the drummer buys a cherry red BMW, the bass player moves out of the practice room over his parents' two-car garage and into a condo, while the keyboard player finds a dealer in specialized pharmaceuticals who has "better connections." So far, so good.

However, in their haste to sign on the dotted line, the Kleptos neglect to read the fine print and overlook the classic rider buried deep in the contract's boiler plate, which obligates them to use only company facilities for recording, mixing, and mastering. A moot point at the time, until they later realize that company facilities are far more expensive than comparable independent ones. (Next time they'll remember to negotiate a separate advance for recording.)

Green but full of hope, they dutifully head off to the company facility, where instead of recording their songs as quickly and efficiently as possible, having worked everything out before hand, they spend countless expensive hours fiddling with the studio's neat effects, tuning the drums, etc. As quick as you can say jumpingjackflash, they've overshot their recording budget. Not to worry, says the in-house producer, as kind and solicitous as can be, you're our artists and we understand your creative process. You just take as much time as you need and we'll work out the details later, trust us. Oy!

In time, a finely crafted cutting-edge piece of pop emerges: The Company product manager and the promotion department think *Slingshot Rumble* will be a monster hit, and they crank up their star-making machine to promote the single "Positive Pain" on radio and in all the music trade magazines. The costs are hefty, especially the under-the-table monies indie promo men unofficially pay to radio station managers to put the single into regional radio market rotation and onto the industry tip sheets that govern them. Though this tactic is nominally illegal, Blitzbomp knows how the game is played; smaller companies or groups who can't afford the "vig" just don't make it. Payola hasn't died, it's just accounted for under another category in the company books.

And so a company-subsidized national promotional tour is arranged, where the group is packaged as an opening act for The Company headliner. Instead of sleeping in Motel 6s they've graduated to Holiday Inns just like real rock stars. Unfortunately, touring isn't all like what it says in *Rolling Stone*. Once expenses are deducted—hotels, meal money, transportation costs, roady salaries, kickbacks to promoters, legal expenses, etc.—there's little left. In that respect they're in the same position as the Rolling Stones, but instead of having Bud Lite or Aramis paying them for product placement, the Kleptos are shilling for The Company and are already well on the way to becoming indentured servants. Every room service steak or extra bucket of ice the band orders on the road just puts them deeper into the hole. Twenty years ago, it was possible to make money on the road—the corporate presence wasn't as pronounced—but now it has become a necessity. Times change. Meanwhile, oblivious to what's about to happen, the band is pumped, enjoying the rush of that first tour. All is going well: They play to packed houses with enthusiastic audiences, The Company is enthusiastic, and the album is briskly selling in the designated markets where the promo men have worked their green magic. Don't worry, be happy, the regional product managers tell them, and 3 furious months later the tour ends.

When the guys return home, psychically bruised but otherwise intact, they learn that not only are they into The Company for a small fortune for the tour but also that the sales of their first CD have already peaked. Additionally, having spent their advance, there's no reserve to cover the recording costs of their second album, whose deadline is fast approaching. Since they had such good response first time out, they decide to go back on the road to produce an album that not only "duplicates the live excitement" of their first tour but also will be padded out with the songs left off their first release. Though the idea sounded good in their living room, the band doesn't realize just how strenuous the road is, even without the additional pressure of writing and recording new material. This plan hinges on the good graces and financial support of The Company and theoretically could work, but meanwhile, because of the lower-than-expected sales figures, Blitzbomp is having second thoughts and decides to reduce its support—a purely hardball business decision.

In fact and more to the point, The Company's A-team of ace publicists and promo men are otherwise engaged in breaking Fruitboy, a Seattle grunge band with potential, who was signed while the Kleptos were on the road; and so its fate is now in the hands of second stringers, trainees, and interns—swell. Since there's less money to spread around, radio airplay slackens. Without the headliner who brought the fannies into the seats last time around, concert grosses decline or gigs are canceled entirely, because whatever audience does show up is smaller now that the band is drawing on its true fans. While the band is on the road, Blitzbomp becomes gradually less available for instant consults; the road manager's phone calls are not returned or returned late. Within the band itself tensions mount; the backstage ambience, formerly so exhilarating, now resembles the movie *This Is Spinal Tap,* a tour bus video favorite the first time around, but not nearly as amusing when it's happening in real life—as the Kleptos are finding out.

The smell of failure is palpable, and everyone knows it: Do not resuscitate this group, please. The second album, rushed out in haste and shoddily produced, is deemed by in-house sources such a colossal stiff that no one wants to be associated with it. Adding insult to injury, the critics, who are hot-wired into the Blitzbomp creative matrix and are smelling blood in the water, jump all over *Live and Flaming,* the new release, and the band for "not living up to its potential," a potential that they weren't given enough time to develop. Sink or swim, that's how it works. It's triage time around The Company headquarters on Hollywood Boulevard, time to pull the plug. The band members aren't even talking to each other. After initial attempts are made to patch things up between the band and The Company, the matter is turned over to the lawyers (hot dog! more bloated fees).

Though the contract can be voided and the group released from its recording obligations, the outstanding debt remains, The Company lawyer sharks inform our lads, who naturally freak out because where are they going to raise that kind of money now since they can't stand the sight of each other? Not to worry, here's the deal, The Company lawyers inform the Kleptos' attorney over sushi: Until the debt has been worked off, we'll retain the rights to use the master recordings and administer—for a fee—the royalties, and when the debt has been discharged, we'll return the tapes to whoever owns them. The band's attorney, a real estate specialist working pro bono as a favor to his brother-in-law, the bass player, brings the deal back to the boys, who are so demoralized, angry, and pissed off at each other that they agree with alacrity and sign off on the deal. Collectively, they figure it's about the best they can get, considering that no matter what kind of advance and press they had, they're still relative nobodies. Onward and upward.

Though the band temporarily may be history in the music press, the group continues to be of economic interest to The Company. With temporary legal possession and control of the master recordings, Blitzbomp can do whatever it sees fit to recoup its initial investment, swollen by the band's additional cost overruns and advances against royalties for the second disastrous and ill-conceived album. Numerous options present themselves: (1) The Company may wholesale the remaining CD stock—for a fraction of the original list price—to independent rack jobbers who service music store and supermarket cut-out bins, clean out their warehouse, and write off the whole thing as a bad investment and move on; (2) or on an in-company budget subsidiary, The Company can repackage the Kleptos on a sampler CD along with other failed bands and sell same at deep discount—with those bands having no creative control over the packaging, cut selection, and even mixing; (3) Blitzbomp can license the masters to other smaller companies who will put out their own package to sell on late night TV—the same creative rules as (3) apply; or (4), sometimes the most prudent and long-term expedient, they can do nothing immediately and wait to see what develops. By letting time and those waves take over and by keeping the album in its backlist catalogue, they can have the money dribble into a special account that, though it can't be directly used by the company (that would be illegal), can produce a tidy collective escrow interest income until it does. Time and those waves work in favor of record companies—why else would they have warehouses full of master tapes of busted bands with unreleased albums? It's possible that after a few years the Kleptos might finally get into the black, but who's going to know unless it's some impossibly ungodly amount of money and their resurrection is just too egregious to ignore? Anyway, the cost of hiring a professional accountant familiar with record business accounting practices to handle the audit are astronomical. By the time he takes his fee, there might not be anything substantial left, live and learn. Heads I win, tails you lose.

But let's say the Kleptos are made of sterner stuff and they sign with another label. Cutting a more equitable and realistic deal with better management and better "chemistry" with the front office, our boys indeed do become bonafide chart busters; it does happen. Or perhaps Brash, our mythical Harvard-MBA moonlighting as the lead guitarist, buys the name of the group from the other members (positive product identification), and with an entirely different personnel plus a horn section makes it big under the same name; same time, next year. If either of these two scenarios eventually present themselves, and the band realizes the potential the original Blitzbomp product manager envisioned but The Company had lacked the patience or vision to see, The Company can theoretically rerelease the original Kleptos material in any form they choose. They can hope there will be some spillover, that at the very least, the rabid fans, or the completists who now fetish the group in all its previous incarnations as a sociological artifact (like the Deadheads who prize how Pigpen played keyboards) will buy all the old stuff just to hear what the band sounded like before it went platinum.

Until that happens, the master recordings of the Kleptos join row upon row, rack upon rack of other master recordings in The Company vaults from bygone days. Like its sister Con-GlomCos back in the late forties and fifties, Blitzbomp recorded and distributed many black blues and r & b singers who also never earned out, but who though they are no longer with the label, continue to earn substantial sums in their repackaged configurations as samplers, as "best of" series. Having long ago forsaken the ways of the white folks, those old r & b cats are still out there on the Chitlin' Circuit making ends meet by distributing their own CDs out of the luggage bays of their battered tour buses; meanwhile their old companies thrive. That's some kind of sociocultural statement in itself, and it cuts to the heart and soul of the music business and the culture that supports it.

Boxers in WalMart?

Music journalists love to write about the struggle of rock stars to attain fame, but they rarely bother to examine the creative consequences of getting famous. About as far as they go in that direction is when they're composing the obits of the ones who O.D. on China White heroin or in the course of making editorial asides in a news story about another poor schnook who declared Chapter Eleven 6 months after his career has peaked and is back on the bar band circuit where he started out so long long ago. Creative politics—if discussed at all—are particularized to specific groups or artists, and rarely are generalizations offered about the nature of the industry as a whole; again it's too close to home. Naturally enough, it's the myths of rock and roll that sell music magazines, not the base truths.

There's a class issue at play: There are *rock stars* and then there are *musicians*, and rarely do their two worlds politically coincide except on stage or in the studio. Within this pleasant prison fiction, rock stars are expected to champion political causes because they're celebrities. Meanwhile, rhythm guitarists, bass players, percussionists, or horn players, the worker bee foot soldiers on whose backs the celebrities stand, the ones who support the rock gods and superstars, are dismissed as virtual nonpersons. We want rock stars and that's what we get, unfortunately. It's better like that, since most musicians are a low-key lot and prefer to keep out of the limelight. With some exceptions, musicians tend to hold liberal or libertarian views if only because they work under all sorts of conditions with all manner of people; to get by to earn a living, they've got to get along. That's the reason professional musicians tend to have "out" senses of humor, why, for instance, David Letterman or Jay Leno, on their late night talk shows, direct all their bad jokes to the band, because the guys have seen and heard it all before. And it really is true: The band sees everything.

Unlike rock stars, musicians have simple needs: (1) they like to play their music and (2) they like to get paid, though they'll play even if they don't get paid. Unscrupulous club owners and managers have exploited this since time immemorial; they know that dedicated musicians will endure the most frightful working conditions just so long as they can express themselves musically and be free for those 15, 45, or 75 minutes on stage. On the other hand, though a rock band may think it's getting paid to musically "tell it like it is" by its fans, once it signs on the dotted line, the record company calls the tune, like it or not. Only in retrospect, after the band becomes part of the music business for a while, does it start to realize just how lucky it was when it was on the outside looking in. Perhaps they learn that those scuffling r & b cats who are no longer actively involved in the system were on to something after all. Even though in their prime these journeymen musicians never made the big time and have been systematically denied their songwriting royalties by the record companies that they served so long and so well, they came away from the whole experience with their creative integrity intact; no mean accomplishment and worth far more than a wall of gold records, a consecutive string of Top 10 hits, or the de rigueur million-dollar beach house that pop music fame buys.

It takes a while for young bands and artists to understand what creative freedom is really all about and that "you've got to suffer to sing the blues." Meanwhile, when music consumers go into a mall music store and are confronted with the racks upon racks of shrink-wrapped CDs, they tend to equate the quantity of merchandise with its quality. Because of this seeming abundance, they think that the musicians and artists who provide them with the soundtracks to their lives create in a perfect world without constraint or censorship of any kind—and of course nothing could be farther from the truth.

In the course of the twentieth century, ragtime, jazz, swing, rock and roll in its infancy, and more recently gangsta rap and hip-hop music have been singled out for artistic censorship by individuals or groups of individuals on behalf of impressionable children or in the name of "family values" and have been subjects for heated political debate on the national, regional, and local levels. Fortunately, free expression of music has been protected under the Constitution's First Amendment, though now it is coming under attack not only from the music industry itself, which is responsible for its production in the first place, but also from the major merchandizing conglomerates who distribute the product. It is an action all the more insidious, because not only is it done in plain sight, but it is also covertly agreed to by the artists themselves. Although the debate about the suitability of hip-hop and gangsta music and lyrics has occupied the discourse of the nineties, the debate was originally framed in its present form in the mideighties when the same issue was raised about heavy metal music.

In 1985, an allegedly bipartisan group of Washington politico wives, who included Susan Baker, the wife of James Baker, Ronald Reagan's State Department head, and Tipper Gore (the vice president's wife and, weirdly enough, a well known bubblegum rock fan), formed the Parents Music Resource Center (PMRC). A lobbying group without dues or members, following the agenda of the Religious Right, the PMRC sent a letter to the president of the Recording Industry of America (RIAA) that accused the industry of exposing youth to "sex, drugs, and the glorification of drugs and alcohol" and proposed that rock and roll records should be rated, though exactly who would do the rating was never specified.

Simultaneously, the PMRC applied pressure on Edward O. Fritts, president of the National Association of Broadcasters, who in turn sent a letter to his members implying that if they broadcast songs with explicit lyrics, they would risk losing their licenses. One of the few musicians to take a public stand on this issue of creative freedom was Frank Zappa. An outspoken rock and classical musician and satirist, Zappa was not only a public critic of the Reagan political agenda but an outspoken critic of the business practices of the music industry as well. For Zappa, the PMRC's public position merely confirmed his own belief "that censorship was turning America into a police state which anyone who'd been listening to his lyrics since the midsixties already knew."[3]

The issue wasn't merely about the content of heavy metal songs, Zappa thought, as much as the radical ideas the music, lyrics, and deportment of the bands conveyed—by which the Reagan White House and the Religious Right (on which its power rested) were threatened. In effect, what this group of well-connected Washington political wives wanted to do was attempt to legislate behavioral norms with a set of implied religious values, which not only violated the Constitution's principle of the separation of church and state but also infringed on free speech. To this end, Zappa mounted a personal campaign where he assailed the PMRC and the agenda of the Religious Right at every and any opportunity, not only from the concert stage, but also on radio and TV talk shows, even including ABC's *Nightline*.[4]

At open hearings held by the Senate Commerce, Technology and Transportation Committee on September 19, 1985, Zappa—along with the unlikely duo of Dee Snyder of the heavy metal band Twisted Sister and John Denver, the country/pop singer of "Rocky Mountain High" fame—testified. Neatly attired in sharp suit and tie, hair neatly combed, Zappa sternly lectured these daughters of moral decency with humor, irony, and intelligence; in a masterful and impassioned performance, he explained how freedom of speech, freedom of religious thought, and the right to due process for composers, performers, and retailers would be imperiled if the PMRC and the major labels went ahead with this sort of legislation.

Though no legislation was ever proposed, on November 1, 1985, the RIAA agreed to voluntarily post warning stickers on politically offending albums with the tag "Explicit Lyrics: Parental Advisory." At the time, compliance was never an industrywide norm, and if it was used at all it was merely as a hip merchandising tool. Of course, with a label like "Parental Discretion Advised," every kid looking for something to piss off his or her parents would naturally be drawn to it, just as buying a book stickered with "Banned in Boston," was another red flag for the bored.

Lucky Zappa's no longer around to see how things have turned out for the First Amendment, especially if one chooses to buy CDs from America's Store, WalMart—as many Americans do. Especially for teenagers with limited funds, there's literally no other place, because WalMart has put out of business many smaller music retailers. For these kids especially, Wal-Mart, "America's Store" where the consumer is king, is the last if not the only best hope. Whatta kingdom, for here the PRMC's agenda thrives. Though it may appear like any other mall store music retailer, general market rules don't apply; WalMart has its own private moral universe.

Contrary to popular belief, not all CDs are available there. The ones that are, the ones that are considered to be sitting on the cusp of acceptability, are "modified" to meet the outlet's definition of "family values." Cover art is crafted not to offend, lyric sheets are edited. On the CDs themselves objectionable lyrics (if not entire tracks) are sometimes electronically masked, reversed, or expunged entirely—especially if the material is really objectionable to WalMart executives. Meanwhile, record companies, because they're in such bad shape these days themselves, instead of refusing to distribute their product to WalMart, go along, because the half loaf is loaf enough—especially with all their overhead. The chilling effect percolates down to apprentice rock and roll bands, who, ever anxious to please but without economic clout, will modify their songs just to get into the WalMart bins. If not the band members themselves, then the producer or the manager leans on them. If a group is intent on moving their product and if the record company wants to stay in the good graces of America's Store, they had best comply with their directives[5] where, in essence, greed's the key.

Corporate censorship also plays a role in the publishing business. It is not uncommon for representatives from the big chains like Waldenbooks or Barnes and Noble to sit on editorial boards to advise publishing houses of a manuscript's "saleability factor." If the big chains don't or won't order the book, no matter how good the title or the subject, the book will be rejected, and to hell with the reader and freedom of speech. Censorship isn't dead; it just smells funny.

In the end it all comes down to that old proverb musicians have: "The more they pay you, the less they want you to play." That goes to the heart of the issue, that interface between music and politics, exactly what the MTV Town Meeting wasn't going to allow either its audience or the candidates to examine in depth. Who would have asked the question? Better, who would have had the ears to listen and hear the answer? The way things are heading these days, pretty soon we won't be allowed our own ears at all.

Boxers? Or briefs?

Chapter 5

Play School

You Can Dress for It, But You Can't Escape It

Recently, while channel-surfing late one night, I caught a pretzel commercial whose setting was a high school reunion where the "Nerd/Dweeb/Grind" gets his revenge. Immediately after being harassed and taunted by his Jock nemesis, our Everyman whips out his secret weapon, a box of pretzels, and after eating a handful like Popeye with his spinach, soundly thrashes the big lug in rope climbing and wrestling, thereby impressing the Cheerleader who never gave him a thought years before. "I think it's the pretzels," confides another Nerd as they both watch the happy couple dancing the night away Disco Fever style.

It was a good piece of work, really, an effective commercial vision, one of many in that vein that to an increasing extent makes up the American cultural landscape these days. Without really meaning to I found myself asking why such a scene was used and why it had so much evocative power (it must have been a good one or I wouldn't have thought about it at all). But more to the point, why was this particular vision in one way or another embedded in the American psyche and continually drawn on as background for innumerable movies, sitcoms, and, especially these days, numerous commercials, for an infinite variety of products? I guess there's a lot to mine there if you are looking, or you still care.

It never changes, does it? Set at least a decade or two after the fact, graduates come back to the smelly old gym to reminisce, comparing notes and dancing to a cheesy band. Wassup? Perhaps the Bad Girl had become a madame (or the Cheerleader, which would go against character but be a twist) or married a power politician; the "Most Likely to Succeed" was very rich or doing 10 to 20 for fraud after having done so illegally at the get-go (served him right, we think); or the Jock, having busted his knee and had a few knocks from life, was mortal like everyone else, etc. Think about it—though living in the present, all these "graduates" still seem prisoners of an adolescent past that has overshadowed any life they've had since.

Is there life after high school? If we live in America and watch television commercials, not really.

High school reunions can be traumatic, no doubt about it: We've got to look our best. Some of us go on crash diets, get a new do (a nose job? liposucton?), new clothes, show up in a stretch limo, possibly all of the above if we're *really* paranoid and self-conscious; some Come Out but most regress entirely. If single perhaps we enlist, entice, or even rent the cooperation, services, and companionship of a dream gal/boy toy for the evening (and who hasn't a clue who the players are); if not, we'll pressure, prep, and spiff up our spouses and significant others to lend some moral support. Some of us may even lie about who we are or what we've become (far easier if we've moved out of town, or the state). Old jealousies flair, old boyfriends/girlfriends reconnect, however briefly; the atmosphere is tense and so are we, and the air around the punch bowl is loud and thick with intrigue or it is pretension as we go through entirely too many changes in the course of the evening.

And even if we boycott the whole business, deep down inside we feel uneasy; obviously the current neologism, "That was then but this is now" doesn't work really, postmodernism to the contrary.

Why does high school still exert such a grip on our emotions and sense of self even when we're safely out of it? The truth is as Parson Weems said of George Washington and the Cherry Tree, "too true to be doubted": We never leave. Oh we may survive it, barely, perhaps—but it dogs our steps forever. And it's no longer just an American peculiarity; for not only is our country awash with adolescent symbolism, but so are the nations of the world who follow America's lead. Indeed, it is this image of adolescence that informs our behavior as well the world's view of us.

Only Americans seem to have this intense investment in their adolescent selves; the rest of the peoples of the world, despite the pervasive influence of American pop culture, still see themselves as developing individuals within a wider perspective, a larger context, culturally and historically. Somehow other cultures get over their adolescence and their minds seem more historically focused and oriented, which in the words of Johan Huizinga, the Dutch historian, "embody in [their] idea of what is 'modern' and 'contemporary' a far larger section of the past than a mind living in the myopia of the moment."[1]

To the contrary: We seem to have no sense at all of our collective historical past, and if we do, we view it with suspicion if we haven't already rewritten it entirely or had a psychiatrist or therapist do so for us. Locked in the myopia of the moment, our idea of continuity can barely be maintained for a week, much less a decade; just look at how the American media reports international "hot spots" when they are "out of the news" for more than a few weeks. When things blow up again, it always comes as a big surprise to us. Generally speaking, most people of the world never have to contend with the trauma of high school reunions, nor do their rituals really lend themselves to such elaborate commercial exploitation, nor would they conceive of movies like *Peggy Sue Got Married* or *American Graffiti*—and maybe never would. Would a Frenchman or a German even think of writing a book called *What Ever Happened to the Class of '65?* Who would read it? And why?

Whence comes this attachment to who we were from the ages of 14 to 18 rather than to what we are, or even who we could become—an attachment so deep that it has become a total world view pervading the very nature of this country's commercial, social, and political interrelationships? Why does this state of expanded adolescence continue to exert such a profound effect on the cultural lives of Americans at the end of the twentieth century, when merely 100 years ago, adolescence and peer group pressure hadn't really been invented and/or commercially exploited and Disney hadn't taken over the world?

Of course high school itself has evolved considerably. What it means today is not what it meant 100 years ago or even 50 years ago, so it's best to define terms, since there are three different kinds of "high school" and adolescent behaviors operative here. First there is the idea of adolescence and the function of high school as explored by G. Stanley Hall, a pioneer psychologist and contemporary of William James and one of the founders of Clark University; second is how Hall's findings and insights were imperfectly interpreted and emasculated by schools of education and professional administrators; and finally, there is the high school of today that administrators have allowed to happen, a society of consumerism and celebrity that feeds a national culture, a candyland of jocks, cheerleaders, fashion jeans, and celebrity journalism all mediated and driven by peer group pressure. Instead of being a rite of passage in an ongoing educational and emotional process, high school has become a terminal state of being for many and has made America into a play school.

In 1907 G. Stanley Hall published *Adolescence*, a seminal two-volume work that straddled the fields of adolescent psychology and education. The work was encyclopedic in its overview, scrupulous in its scholarship; Hall showed himself to be a fearsomely well-read and erudite advocate of "humanism" in the care and feeding of the sometimes contrary, testosterone-driven, and, these days, headbanging/party-hardy teenager of common contemporary literary currency. Hall's view of *pubescesis americanus* was more benign and transcendent, less consumer-driven. To his mind, the adolescent awakens to a new world and understands neither it nor himself [where] character and personality are taking form, but everything is plastic. Self-feeling and ambition are increased, and every trait and faculty is liable to exaggeration and excess. It is all a marvelous new birth, and those who believe that nothing is so worthy of love, reverence and service as the body and soul of youth, and who hold that the best test of every human institution is how much it contributes to bring youth to the very fullest possible development, may well review themselves and the civilization in which we live to see how far it satisfies this supreme test.[2]

For such an individual, a nurturing, empowering educational system was vitally necessary because "youth needs repose, leisure, art, legends, romance, idealization, in a word humanism, if it is to enter the kingdom of man well equipped for man's highest work in the world."[3] Consequently, Hall argued, a new breed of teacher must emerge who was able to initiate students into the mysteries of the universe rather than a drillmaster transmitting information by rote memorization.[4] It was in adolescent youth that Hall saw the hope of mankind and its traditions:

Youth when properly understood, will seem to be not only the revealer of the past but of the future, for it is simply prophetic of that best part of history which is not yet written because it has not yet transpired, of the best literature the only criterion of which is that it helps to an ever more complete maturity, and of better social organizations, which, like everything else, are those that best serve youth.[5]

(On the whole, this seems to be a more elevating alchemic description of a teacher's function than that of pencil counter, disciplinarian, or study hall monitor, no? And it's a far more desirable occupation than being a shuttlecock, bereft of the authority to teach what and how they know best, in the badminton match between their union, school administrators, parent/ teacher groups, and politically ambitious school boards, not to mention the test scorers and their brokers. Maybe it's all that can be expected in a society that grossly underpays and undervalues its teachers and their contributions and where students, by and large, mimicking society's low opinion of their jobs in the "real world," don't give them any respect either. Compared to the lures of celebrity, fame, and money, the teacher's life is, well, pale. You poor sap, they think, can't you do better, can't you make something of yourself and make some *real* money?

To Hall's mind, the high school philosophy that would serve youth best was one that provided "evolution, not revolution, grafting and not uprooting, a revival of the best in them in this best age and not a fanatical running amuck."[6] Though these thoughts and aspirations still have considerable resonance today and lip service is paid to his theories (excerpts from his book are required reading for educational psychology students). *Adolescence* is rarely ever read and studied in its entirety because the prospect of slogging through 1700 closely reasoned Whitmanesque pages of prose is a daunting prospect. So much the worse for the state of American education.

It's true that Hall's conception of adolescent education and adolescents seems a bit idealistic to our modern sensibilities, but it was positive. However, at the end of the nineteenth and beginning of the twentieth centuries, for intellectually challenged run-of-the-mill administrators and bureaucrats in the nascent field of education fighting for respect with the disciplines of sociology and psychology, his ideas posed considerable policing and control problems. And as administrators have done from time immemorial when challenged by complex thoughts, they sought to reduce his ideas to technology and "science" that focused largely on mechanics rather than on his underlying philosophy. Hall was horrified at how rote learning and mindless memorization had already disfigured the educational process and how administrators had encouraged and produced teachers whose methodology was to

> dissect large living wholes, which pubescents crave, into elements, which they abhor . . . [in a system that involves] logic

chopping, formal steps, analysis of processes that should never
be analyzed, or overexplanation . . . [which blunts] the intuitions,
the best thing of youth. . . . More, it tends to pedantry that
shields ignorance from exposure, teaches the art of seeming
wise with empty minds, brings complacency that tends to arrest
in the teacher, and whips up a modicum of knowledge to decep-
tive proportions.[7]

If they couldn't blind with brilliance, they'd baffle students
with bullshit, no?

It was also Hall's belief that high school should not be
scholiocentric but *pediocentric:* one taught from the point of
view of inspiring students. Teachers were there to facilitate
learning and not as tools or guinea pigs for whatever trendy educational philosophy was being pushed by their administrators.

Formerly voluntary, compulsory secondary education by
the twenties was mandated for all regardless of abilities or proclivities. Though on the surface a step forward, the overall result
for thinkers like historian Richard Hofstader, among others,
from the vantage point of the early sixties was that

secondary school pupils were not merely unselective but also
unwilling; they were in high school not because they wanted further study but because the law forced them to go. The burden of
obligation shifted accordingly; whereas once the free high
school offered a priceless opportunity to those who chose to
take it, the school now held a large captive audience that its administrators felt obliged to satisfy . . . [resulting in] schools filled
with a growing proportion of doubtful, reluctant, or actually hos-
tile pupils.[8]

In truth, Hall's ideas were either imperfectly and shabbily
grafted onto the developing system or ignored altogether; high
school principals and school boards, instead of being educators,
became custodians in the entertainment business, in effect
shifting their attention away from those who wanted to learn to
those who had little desire. As high school attendance rose in

the forties and fifties the idea of a "life adjustment" curriculum to cope with this influx of the willing and the unwilling came into educational vogue, which, according to Hofstader "gear[ed] the educational system more closely to the needs of children who were held to be in some sense uneducable."[9] This gave the definitive boot to Hall's notion that there was a basic body of knowledge upon which *all* students could focus *whatever* their individual gifts. Instead of a positive view of youth, secondary education focused on the negative systemwide assumption that "in a system of mass secondary education, an academically serious training is an impossibility for more than a modest fraction of the student population."[10]

The ensuing result has been disastrous as well as predictable, since the "life adjustment" curriculum was aimed

> not primarily to fit them [high school students] to become a disciplined part of the world of production and competition, ambition and vocation, creativity and analytical thought, but rather to help them learn the ways of the world of consumption and hobbies, of enjoyment and social compliance—*in short to adapt gracefully to the passive and hedonistic style summed up in the significant term adjustment* [emphasis mine].[11]

Considering that the advertising industry had already launched a major effort to define and exploit the burgeoning teenage market of the fifties, this was hardly news. In truth they'd been working for the previous 60 years on ways to commercially exploit the research findings of Progressive educators like G. Stanley Hall and John Dewey, who'd been doing similar studies on adolescent behavior but for less mercenary ends.*

It's also not surprising that this trend continues today and that a recent study by the National Commission on Time and

---

*For an extraordinarily detailed, informed, and acutely observed history of merchandizing in America, see William Leach's *Land of Desire: Merchants, Power and the Rise of a New American Culture* (New York: Pantheon Books, 1993).

Learning discovered that high school teachers spend only 41% of their time on academic subjects[12] while the remainder is occupied by nonacademic subjects like drivers' ed, sex education, home economics, self-esteem courses, special interest clubs, study hall, or writing reports on who was accountable to whom for what.

Now we are up to speed, since the modern high school was essentially a creature of the fifties. It was here that the newly discovered economic clout of the teenage market was added to what had been since the twenties an age-segregated universe. When the two converged with the "life adjustment" curriculum, an adolescent consumer kingdom was created. And though the school administrators may have convinced themselves they were following Hall's pediocentric principles, they were in effect opening a marketplace that offered students the freedom to choose what *they wanted* to learn (simultaneously keeping them content and occupied until age 18), not what they should learn, which would have opened them to the educational possibilities of a lifetime. Instead of a place where one learned how to learn, high school became a vocational institution that parents and communities demanded and expected because it was easily quantifiable and utilitarian. Industrial arts students learned industrial arts, college-track learned liberal arts, and so on, though both (all) could have benefitted from a knowledge of the other's field. Instead of providing tools to seek answers or lifetime long-term learning strategies, high school promoted (and to a large extent continues to provide now) short-term answers for long-term questions, i.e., how to pass *the test* (college boards, etc.) that gives the appearance of having mastered knowledge. This is a weakness that contemporary colleges are paying dearly for since it takes almost 2 years for high school "graduates" to get up to speed for higher education. As a result, teachers having by default given up the function of being initiators of learning became administrators of entertainment programs if they were lucky, or enforcers of penal colony study halls if they were not.

"Twenty years of schooling and they put you on the day shift" may have been an ironical comment voiced by Bob Dylan to the generation of the sixties, but for the temp's life in downsized America today it has even more validity. College or grad school notwithstanding, the one thing that ties multicultural America together is that everyone goes to high school, and for better or worse, that's where we all learn about the franchise that America now represents to the world. Once safely out of its clutches, unless we are essentially flunking high school with pay in our jobs, the experience tends to be mercifully and quickly forgotten, glossed over and buried, or at the very least protected by a hard mental calculus.

We chuckle about it uneasily when confronted with the inevitable pictorials in periodicals from *People* to *Esquire* to *Rolling Stone,* those grainy yearbook miniatures of the superjocks, glamourpusses, egregious axe-murderers, former cheerleaders turned stock swindlers, or even billionaire techno-nerds in all their geekiness or glory. Yes, we think to ourselves, even "they" had to endure high school just like the rest of us mortals, the spear carriers, the walk-on players who endured like Faulkner's Dilsey in the background. Seeing them the way they were makes us all feel a little better, but why? When it's all said and done, what did we learn, those of us who haven't totally repressed the whole business?

For students then and now the song remains the same: You can dress for it, but you can't escape it. It's so much a part of our experience that the wry observation "Hollywood is high school with money"[13] is understood by all with a wince of recognition. What is a no-brainer to any kid paradoxically escapes the most articulate and committed educator, to wit: It's not so much what goes on in the classroom that makes high school *high school,* but what goes on before or after school, in the halls changing classes, in the lunch room, in the gym, or out on the ball fields. And as long as there isn't a riot in the hallways and the natives aren't restless, administrators don't want to deal with what comes in to the school as much as the stats for certifying what comes out of it to someone else. Principals and school board members hardly ever change; students do, continually. It's protean world out there, an ever-shifting universe for the average freshmen to see the parade of one's peers, a place previously described by historian Gilbert Ostrander (see Chapter 2), where," No sooner have the rules of the game been officially explained by the younger generation, than another game is discovered to be in progress on the same field under different rules by a somewhat different younger generation."[14]

And you never catch up to any of it (nor are you supposed to).

It's painful, it bites the big one, if you could die and somehow graduate, that would be fine, too; still, everyone agonizes(ed) over learning the right intricate dance steps and moves. Essentially, it is a period, in the words of E. Z. Friedenberg, "during which a young person learns who he is, and what he really feels. It is the time during which to differentiate himself from his culture, though on the culture's terms."[15] It is also the first universe youth experience outside of the safe confines of home (aside from the toy merchants on TV) and the comparative safety of one teacher and one homeroom. Age-segregated, insular, and self-referential, it is a total universe where one is provided with an identity of a peer group that "takes over where the individual student–school dynamics leave off."[16] In this unforgiving and merciless universe, style is more important than content, and one learns the weight of outward appearance and social rituals that, though extrapolated from mainstream culture, are filtered through the prism of an adolescent angst that completely skews one's perspective; truly it is "the received world experienced as the only world."[17]

And even this would be fine if it were a developmental stage rather than a feedback loop, but it's not, and perhaps here's why:

It is not only the present generation of high school students "moving off the field and trying to stay on the field by turning into something else" who are involved, but also nearly 85% of all Americans who've gone through high school since the fifties, including the original "teenage market" that Madison Avenue exploited, for whom high school is never far away, and our spirit, like Marley's ghost, lingers in the halls nonetheless. As fifties' teenage concerns were serviced by a variety of specialized goods and "our class" moved out of high school into college and eventually into "the real world," we were statistically identified, coded, and tracked, subsequently to be offered more "adult" versions of the same goods that animated our desires and defined our "coolness" (or lack thereof) back then. It is the same mechanism that has evolved into a powerful and efficient merchandizing machine, the model for how future generations were to be commercially exploited. Now high school generations, instead of being considered 4 years long, are only 2 years long, thanks to sophisticated marketing techniques that have promoted homogenization of tastes through overdiversification. What was once a paradox is now a TV given, for not only are school-age children and young adults encouraged to keep up, but so are the rest of us encouraged to maintain the "edge" advertisers tell us we are in danger of losing. Each successive high school "generation" has only refined the franchise's nuances; in truth, Ostrander's observation describes one of the mechanisms by which American markets have been exploited over time.

It's been going on for almost 50 years, from the ubiquitous Saturday morning cartoon–toy tie-ins to the ever-glamorous Lite beer MTV teen world of today, so much a part of our consciousness we don't even notice it anymore. It's a given: Whatever styles brew in the hormonal soup of high school eventually will wind up in *Vogue*. And though definitions of what constitutes "cool" may change from generation to generation (i.e., every 2 years), we are all led to believe that our need to maintain our "edge" remains constant. Which is

what the franchise has banked on anyway, and they've succeeded in getting us all by the short hairs whether we want to
admit it or not.

High school has devolved into a climate-controlled social
and cultural environment in which one is encouraged to try
on various off-the-shelf lifestyles (be they costumes, attitudes,
poses, identities, etc.) provided by consumer society. Instead
of a place to develop individual maps, it has become primarily
a place where the collective assimilation of peer values is
taught. It would be a fairer fight, a more transcendent journey,
if the maps came from a variety of sources and age perspec-
tives.

If everything is brokered and judged solely in terms of
style over substance, especially self-knowledge, that's big
trouble. When consumerism is promoted as a quick and pain-
less fix to get through adolescence, it's disastrous unless
everyone is willing to remain defined by the high school game.
And who among us has not thought how wonderful life would
have been if somehow we all managed to avoid it entirely, high
school and adolescence?* By this quick palliative the consumerist mind-set legitimizes and promotes early and at a highly
impressionable age the rule of the "cult of the new." Students
are the priests, while the fashion brokers advertise themselves as
the only and preferred authority (or a more seductive one than
boring adult retrospective wisdom) for many crucial "teenage"
decisions. Thus seamlessly have the brokers neatly harnessed
the "myth of progress" to the myth of the "Endless Summer"
working up an appealing notion that sells everything from beer,
hamburgers, and automobiles to coordinant lifestyles and foreign policies (but that's another matter entirely). While por-

----

*It may be fashionable these days to dismiss the notion of "storm and stress"
in adolescent development as irrelevant or old-fashioned, but I suspect those
who do don't have any teenagers around the house or haven't really talked to
them if they do.

traying itself to youth as a benign, largely apolitical, neutral
public service providing an all-purpose series of maps for
guiding youth on its journey to "adulthood," consumerism has
actually supplied youth (and the rest of us too) with relative and
contradictory maps the meaning of which it controls and that
are dependent on the value of its goods alone.

As goods become ideas and students become habituated
to the ever-changing panorama of prepackaged images, they become easier to manipulate, and a kind of mindless goods-
enforced conformity is elevated and encouraged. In the end,
this process runs contrary to the idea that adolescence is a period of "growth and individuation [which] can be fruitful only if
a reasonable and increasing degree of integrity is maintained."[18]
These days, there is no chance to discover that integrity, since
the ideas themselves have none in real time. A spurious kind of
integrity is substituted instead, far easier to comprehend and infinitely interchangeable as fancy (and/or fashion) dictates—
which superficially appeals to a teenager's desperate need to
know. The pace and cost of this kind of change has exacted a
heavy price, not only for those in the system now but also for all
the rest of us who survived it.

The bottom line, of course, is what novelist, essayist, and
humorist Kurt Vonnegut observed more than two decades
ago: "that life is nothing *but* high school." And the reason has
as much to do with the quality of high school life today as with
how the quality of American life has changed or has been at-
rophied. In truth, we are never far removed from the high
school experience because the brokers are constantly reinventing it with television shows like *Welcome Back Kotter* or
Saved by the Bell or *Beverley Hills 90210* or movies that range
in budget and/or attitude from *Blackboard Jungle* through
the films of John Hughes (*Sixteen Candles*, *The Breakfast
Club*), *Fast Times at Ridgemont High*, and *Bill and Ted's Ex-
cellent Adventure*, to *Weird Science*, *Clueless*, and *Romy and
Michelle's High School Reunion*. And while those presently in

"the big house" chuckle knowingly at exquisitely observed details (the command of contemporary slang, the clothes, etc.), the rest of us wipe our sweaty brows and heave a sigh of relief, as though we're afraid we never really leave, and there's the rub. So—what song remains? Whose was it? Was it real—or Memorex after all?

For us as individuals, retrospective reediting of memory's tapes or nostalgia's healing properties coupled with some semblance of productive post-high school life will perhaps help to assuage those old feelings, and we may succeed at the very least in rewriting the whole business. Perhaps we can exorcise the memory of being in a total environment controlled for the most part by teachers who were marking time and making do or flashbacks of chuckle-headed principals and assistant principals and phys ed teachers who themselves were working out their own high school disappointments on you and yours eternally. (Ain't that the truth?) Then what? How does America deal with its collective tapes? Where do we begin ? Whose rules were lodged? Which games did we all learn how to dodge?

135

Here's what it is: If instead of accepting, making do, or settling for their designated identities as consumers, market makers, and/or omniscient spectators, high school students lived more within the world instead of out of it in age-segregated and peer-mediated environments, they'd be able to effect real societal change. By living in the present with a presence of the past they would cease to be mere bellwethers for transient consumer preferences whose future identity was to be inevitably homogenized as items on their own nostalgia futures market down the road, a statistical blip. Instead of being a symptom of the problem, the linchpin that eternally ties them and us all into the consumer society, they'd become part of the solution, and we'd all have a chance to break the loop.

As it stands, high school is a far cry from the environment G. Stanley Hall had envisioned for youth (and eventually for all

Americans). For students in its grip today there is no time for "repose" amidst the crush of extracurricular activities, while "art, legends, romance, and idealization" are now supplied by ABC/Disney. As for the "kingdom of man"—for which the adolescent should have been "well-equipped for man's highest work in the world"—that has become the art of knowing how and when to buy discount Air Jordans at the mall. Jeez.

Chapter 6
The Twinkie Defense

The defendant is innocent of murder by reason of diminished capacity brought on by eating too many Twinkies.

—Judicial reason for acquittal of Dan White for the murders of San Francisco Mayor George Moscone and City Supervisor Harvey Milk, 1978

Recently my wife and I attempted our semiannual clean-up/edit of our children's room—more specifically, their toy box caches, which periodically overflow, threatening the sanity and general safety of our home. We have four under the age of 12: two girls, plus twin boys. God love 'em all, so there's an extraordinary amount to rifle through in the short period of time when the children are asleep at a decent hour (*when* is also problematic as those with young children can attest).

If the purge is done ineptly, whatever you throw out, if not decisively hidden, will find its way back inside; if done craftily, by the time they find out they're missing that three-wheeled car that invariably winds up on the staircase to trip you up their attention will be taken up by a new Something That Everyone Everywhere Has—there's always another movie with another burger promotional tie-in that eventually turns up underfoot, stuffed into sofa cushions, or tossed under the seats of the baby-mobile for you to find months later. It appears that in franchise food America, there are endless vistas of disposable plastic gew-gaws to look forward to. Glasses with logos are a whole other matter; we've got a cupboard of these "plastic refugees"; though shatter-proof and prone to cloud up after machine washing, they have somewhat more utility, though the day is rapidly approaching when that space will be liberated and they too will exit, stage right, into the garbage. It's not that they aren't nice enough, and even useful; some of them are even artful. It's just that I don't like being hyped while I'm eating; enough's enough already.

Nevertheless, while our children slept, having crashed early for a change, we diligently and frantically worked our way through the accumulated rubble of promotional toys, the busted and damaged plastic action figures, testaments to our numerous trips to the franchise burgerterias of western Massachusetts, the accumulated receipts from our worship and attendance on the altar of fast food America. It proved an exhaustive and instructive trip down memory lane (of course we had all the videotapes), from *The Little Mermaid* to *Aladdin* to *Beauty and the Beast* to *Batman*, plus there were others that neither of us could identify from *temps perdu*. And so while mucking out my children's Augean stables, it seemed to me at least that the fast food franchise business was no longer even concerned with selling convenience food and had turned into just another outlet for promotional goods, that their true business was to continually add to my children's mythopoetic midden heaps or the plastic refugee closet. In fact there were so many of them it is hard to tell which campaign came with what figure (or maybe all too apparent), and at that point I started thinking about fast food in America, how America eats and goes home, and what.

In 1983 *Blue Highways*, a quirky American road trip travelogue written by William Least Heat Moon, was a national bestseller. A satisfying leisurely read, it was an eye-opening meander into and around the heartland of America, as much about the varieties of roadside food found off the interstate as the individuals he met and places he passed through. In his circumnavigation of the United States, Moon encountered and sampled a variety of culinary experiences in the Great Unknown—some good, some bad, and some inedible—but throughout his odyssey, he followed the Traveling Salesmen's Golden Rule: If in doubt, *cherchez le truckstop diner*. After all, diners don't stay in business long if they don't satisfy the customers. In the course of the book, Moon developed for himself (and his readers) a kind of folk diner taxonomy, a classification system further fine-tuning the maxim: While invariably every diner has a calendar beside or above the cash register, the better ones had two, but the really extraordinary legendary ones had three—for no good reason really, it just was.

Sitting with Moon in the booth at these three-, two-, or one-calendar diners, the reader also waxes nostalgic and wonders how this formerly thriving "counterculture," with its unique regional specialties, pies, cakes, and breakfast specials, has been slowly fading away, smothered and displaced by franchise and mall culture, how even our patterns of eating have altered. The pace of contemporary society doesn't encourage us to linger over coffee and donuts and pie anymore, and the uniquely regional variations of food we used to take for granted are being replaced by the glossy pictures of junk food hamburgers that have displaced the calendars in franchise palaces.

Before the Golden Arches and the interstates, America used to be a land of uniquely regional roadside stands, each with its own spirit, character, and tastes mirrored in the burgers, shakes, hot dogs, hoagies, submarines, sundaes, and the like served. The diners may have been truck stop oases, breakfast clubs, high school hangouts, or morning community coffee klatch stops, and they functioned as community meeting places after the prom, the football or basketball game, or the movies. The service may have been fast or indifferent; the food itself may not have been so great, but the community feeling was there, and that's what counted. (Of course there were those kinds of places where everything was really horrible, including the coffee, but they survived because they were the only place to hang.) The point that Moon was getting at was that what was a matter for individual taste and preference has over time become an interchangeable industrial component.

141

Once upon a time long ago and far away in America, there used to be a daily social ritual called "dinnertime," still available in grainy electronic simulation and 5-minute video bites in netherworlds of the sitcomland of Nickelodeon, the Nostalgia Channel, or FX. Before we had it "our way" out, dinnertime took place when families sat down to eat the evening meal. Depending on one's age and abilities, everyone pitched in so that at a stated time (5 to 6:30, perhaps) all could sit down to be debriefed and discuss the remains of the day, probably the main time when the family interacted as a unit.

That was superseded by the ritual of the "TV" dinnertime of the late fifties when people sat around the old tube with prepackaged individualized food portions and more or less did (or tried to do) the same thing, depending what was on and who had control of the buttons on the console (or the clicker). Though less labor-intensive for Mom, Sis, Junior, or Dad (if he was trying to be helpful around the house by scoring a few points and maybe get lucky with Mom after the kids went to bed), the lowly TV dinner still required a moderate sense of timing, some personal attention. With the rise of the two-working-parent family and the phenomenon of latchkey kids, dinnertime has receded into memory, replaced by take-out, which may or may not accomplish the same family thing.

However, if we believe the incessant barrage of advertising (virtually impossible to avoid in any media), modern families on the go prefer meeting in Burgerland rather than even eating take-out at home because no one can be bothered to cook (microwaving, or "nuking," counts in this psychology) or clean up; it's just too time-consuming and tedious, however short order. "I want it now and I don't want to think about it" is the prevailing fast food philosophy. Included along with the food, of course, is the "wholesome family environment," so about the only thing that these marvelous multicultural oases don't provide are beds (but we all know that's coming). However, even under the best circumstances the ambiance is harried; what with all those microwave bells and the pinging of the fry cookers, it sounds almost like a hospital emergency room, not the place for more than a refuelling stop. No one lingers as one did in a real old-fashioned diner, and those who do are the desperate and the homeless—eat and go, not come and eat, that's what we all do.

But then again, "dining" is not the fast food experience, nor was it intended to be.

If function ultimately supplants form and technology inexorably marches onward, as it seems inexorably and regularly to be doing, crafty food technologists some day soon will, by dint of a strong and persuasive advertising campaign, convince us that even the dubious pleasure of eating in these burgerlands will be deemed unfashionable. In their incessant selfless struggle to service their public's fetish for convenience, promoted in its place will be the far handier, more instantaneous and time-efficient cost-effective expedient of pill-popping; or for people with more time on their hands, just hooking up the 'ole IV to a designated port; best believe the Internet junkies have that concept hotwired and already on-line. Soon hamburger midnights with or without the family will be history, along with all that touchy-feely family stuff that's freighted with the pitch now too. Nor will anyone cook at home; it will be just a place to crash.

The result of course is that progress will be served while at the same time ethnic, regional, and eventually family cooking traditions and the accompanying lore will be forgotten. Instead of Mom's home cooking, it's Miguel's down the block. Instead of the home being the focal point of family life, it will be the franchise, which will result in more families imploding or self-destructing, and consequently people will get more crazy and alienated from each other than they apparently already are. They won't know why they are, but we who are watching this phenomenon take hold will, won't we? But let's not move too quickly here; rather, let us rest for the moment in this present time and space while that scenario is momentarily unthinkable. Yes, we think to ourselves as we bus our trays and return to our so-called lives, that definitely hit the spot, now what about some real food?

This is not to diss the individually prepared and attention-lavished backyard burger or the odd roadburger Out There.

Rather, we are examining those that are mass-produced by the millions or consumed by the sackful. It's an operative consideration to note again that though the former may take a little longer to prepare and serve, you *can* really have it your way instead of theirs. And the trick the franchises have pulled off big time is they've made us (and the world) think that "their way" *is* ours (or yours) through the incessant barrage of advertising. Magnificently and professionally they have succeeded in creating a total universe they control, one that isn't merely confined to what's on the menu either. What does this junk food fascination really say about us? What does this experience promote and project?

We're not talking about other fast food like fast-fried chicken, pizza, barbecued ribs, sushi deluxe, or an overstuffed dripping pita—though all are consumed with relish and are fast enough to be fast food but not the "real thing." There's something ineluctably inalienable and utterly unique about the franchise fastburger—as any true aficionado knows—which is akin to mainlining heavy drugs. It's so sublime, so satisfying, that instantaneous unmistakable hit, the rush that takes place when the stomach's former void is decisively nullified, and temporarily one feels at peace with the world; there can be no equivalent, no substitutions permitted. It's universes away from the feeling that the English have when "peckish" for something to eat—a term way too specific, effete, and delicate, since it implies there's some deliberative process at work that is based on the operant consideration that one has the ability, nay, the leisure, to pick and choose what one wants to eat on the spur of the moment; there's a delicious feeling of discerning indecisiveness in the term, no?

Au contraire—in American burgerspace, instinct prevails; thinking has nothing to do with it, it's a gestural characteristic of Americans that one surrenders enthusiastically and obliviously, inhaling in seeming seconds a junkburger with all the trimmings and fries, washing it all down with the franchise-approved carbonated, flavored water. In the ultimate present tense of "eat," this is all well and good, but (and this is a big *but* for some) somewhere between three-quarters of an hour to an hour and a half later comes the inevitable aftermath, the afterburn, when gastrointestinal juices attempt to decode the latest substance without sustenance one has instinctively and with no malice aforethought (or any thought, for that matter) ingested. As with any archetypical junk food experience, said digestive process will in fits and starts continue throughout the remainder of the day as if to remind us of what our baser instincts have made us do. We always tell ourselves we'll go for the salad next time, but we forget. Anyway, didn't that burger look good?

More to the point, didn't the food pictured over the cash register (or in the TV advert) look mouth-watering, which is what we think we're eating? And it damned well better look good, if we'd spent the millions the burger boys have on food stylists who transform the product to make it look scrumptious after sitting under the hot klieg lights for hours and hours for those product shoots; it's a miracle there's anything even remotely organic left to photograph, but it looks good, and that's the point. (One remarks in passing that the Japanese, when viewing the artful plaster of Paris representations of sushi in the windows of their restaurants, are in no way laboring under the delusion that what they see will be what they'll eat quite in the same way; to them, art is art and eat is eat, though perhaps they're responding to the art in the Golden Arches, who knows?)

145

Here each time we go into the burgerteria we somehow forget that this is the case and then become disappointed and dispirited when the apparent 6-inch tall delish-looking wonder-burger is less than one and a half, wilted and squashed when unwrapped, but then again the Japanese are still an inscrutable people.

Now everybody can eat American junk food. It's inevitable, the quintessential American franchise experience one no longer needs to be American to enjoy; just ask the ravenous crowds in Moscow, Bejing, or Tokyo who are scarfing down Big Macs and Whoppers in record numbers these days. The former bête noir of fusty leftists, Coca-Cola imperialism has long since been eclipsed, decisively supplanted by burger madness, that international fondness for the American franchise fastburger, a new form of benign multicultural nationalism less socially threatening and, to the modern sensibility, of little consequence.

In World War II, our boys may have promoted Europe's love for Spam, and during the Vietnam era, Coke was it, the Real Thing that taught the world to sing. The "Cola Wars" continue as the Cold War has ended, and for good, one hopes, and now we Americans seem to have it "our way" just like the jingle promises; but whose way is that? In a few short decades since our collective national perspective has "evolved" yet again, today it's an unremarkable fact that in the late fifties when then-Vice President Richard Nixon, a designated point man and "agent of godless imperialism" for the Cold War, went to Russia for his famous "kitchen debate" with Premier Khrushchev, he was simultaneously acting as a middleman for Pepsi Cola to broker distribution rights throughout the mighty Soviet Union.

Cola politics has taken on a greater significance these days, for at a Russian–American summit meeting that coincided with the 50th anniversary of the end of World War II, President Bill Clinton was photographed drinking a Coke (horrors!) instead of a Pepsi brokered in the dark Nixonian past. American political and diplomatic observers were quick to divine this act's significance: A sign of the times of shifting power, they concluded, since Pepsi was a "Republican" drink while Coke was the beverage preferred by Democrats—a pointed observation of questionable veracity if there ever was one, for political historians to divine at some future date. It's probably more the case for Clinton of grabbing what was close, cold, and wet, since mineral water doesn't really hit the spot and liquid potato, unless one is habituated to its taste, doesn't satisfy after a hard day of speci-

fying on the international stage—though it may dull the pain
somewhat.

These days, vice presidents don't have the clout they used
to have (or maybe never really did) in international affairs, since
American fast food multinationals routinely bypass the federal
government and deal directly with premiers and finance ministers abroad. Ironically (and this age is big on irony), setting up a
bottling plant and a distribution network is a comparatively
small investment as opposed to what McDonald's has done in
the former Soviet Union. Not only did it provide the architec-
tural blueprints for the Big Mac outlets themselves but also the
economic agricultural R & D so that their Russian business partners could be supplied the requisite grade beef and vegetables
when their native produce proved too variable, unsuitable, and
substandard.

A further irony is that though this simple act of franchise-
building commerce may appear on the surface to be less diplo-
matically pernicious than building another aggressive-looking
high-tech listening post in the middle of nowhere, its effect on
the host country's national and cultural integrity is far more insidious and pronounced. (Naturally one wonders just how
many spooks are working their Russian McJobs under Agency
sponsorship, but that's a thought too bizarre to contemplate . . .
for now, isn't it?) But that's what the McDonald's Corporation
did (the franchise, not the McSpook interns) with their money,
and all so their Big Macs will taste as if they came hot off the
griddle in Peoria. Though seen as a contemporary consumer
miracle for the postmodern age and yet another indication of
how interconnected we all have become, it is also highly paradoxical how much more effective their franchise has been in
"winning the Cold War." What Lend/Lease, grain and commodity deals, or the budget-killing Star Wars boondoggle programs failed to achieve, McDonald's and Burger King have
done without killing anyone in the process (a debatable sidebar,
as any French cultural nationalist will explain). It's really true

that though the world may yet have problems swallowing the concept of representative democracy, few countries will refuse the pleasure of an all-beef patty slathered with mustard, ketchup, lettuce, and special sauce for its people, consumers all. How come?

Junk food is not peculiar to America or Americans, God knows; we're not the only people who like finger food or eating on the run. Any international traveler knows the English have their fish and chips, the French their crepes, the Russians their blintzes, the Chinese their noodle stands, the Japanese their yakitori, the Indonesians their satay, the Middle Eastern countries their kebabs and falafel, as well as the South Americans their tacos and burritos, etc. And so we encounter all of them either in mildly spiced forms in mall land or full-strength in ethnic enclaves in any large or medium-sized city. Getting good eats isn't the issue here; exactly what we're really eating is.

So it's great happy business for the burger kings that everyone just everywhere loves their food, but ignored and overlooked in this worldwide feeding frenzy are far larger questions: Is the demand based solely on the product itself or on what the product stands for? What possesses hearty Muscovites to queue for hours just to spend close to a day's salary on something that costs us a fraction of that amount and that we as Americans take for granted (if we take it at all)? Could it be due to the iconographic packaging that subliminally appeals, or is it perhaps yet another example of the truism that you are what you eat, itself some mad blasphemous parody of That Supper where Christ advised his disciples, "Do this in remembrance of me" and the ubiquitous Big Mac is transformed into an alchemic wafer, an edible vehicle for the transubstantiation of life in these United States? If so, are ancillary citizenship rights or privileges of which we are not aware magically appended thereto? Does the appearance of Marlboro T-shirts, Coca-Cola rally caps, or Warner Brothers cartoon jackets also activate such marvelous visions of our "off-the-shelf" lifestyle? Is this junkfood-ization of world culture the mechanism by which democracy is to be promoted and extended? The ultimate Trojan Horse? I mean, why is there really something so overwhelmingly comforting and satisfying, so ineluctably necessary that the junk food experience (save for the small change) remains invariant, so that the burger one eats in Paris, Rome, Kuwait, or London tastes as though it came from right off the interstate in Anymall U.S.A.?

And while attempting to digest our mythburger we have plenty of time to consider just how representative it is of modern life in these United States while simultaneously noting to our astonishment just how prophetic Johan Huizinga's comments on America were in the twenties (see Chapter 1), how he himself may unknowingly have been the patron philosopher of franchises like McDonalds, Wendy's, or Burger King when he characterized the American experience as "This, Here, Soon"—the junkfood mantra. Not only do we expect our burgers (ourselves?) to be instantaneous, filling, and of a known quantity, but we expect the same from every other commodity, from washing machines to cars to Q-tips (and we're habituated to the inevitable merchandizing tie-ins as well, with brand-name iconography on the rally jackets, T-shirts, and baseball caps, too). To have those expectations with consumer goods is one thing, but we get into serious trouble when we do so with social and political ideas by marketing them with the same panache, brio, and industrial efficiency as Whoppers (the metaphorical burger, not the familiar name for prevarications—you know, big lies?).

149

Every current event seems the stuff of fast food roadburgers these days; we are reminded daily that we live in an in-your-face age where regularly (regular?) diverse sociopathologic miscreants of the criminal, financial, and political kind hide in plain sight. Voyeuristically we look on as they are captured, tried, convicted, and/or exonerated with dismal regularity in expensive show trials. Too shell-shocked or desensitized to care, we become cynical or go into denial as we look for someone to blame, while feeling irresistibly entertained as the titillating stories are regularly turned into movies of the week, some stories whose ashes are barely cold, like the federal botch of the Branch Davidian shoot-out in Waco, Texas, a few years ago. Or the now-mythic O.J. Bronco slow-pursuit convoy on the freeways of Los Angeles, watched by millions coast-to-coast on network and cable TV and invested with exhaustive expository insights delivered in *New Yorker* magazine and *Esquire* with photos by Annie Liebowitz or Richard Avedon, incredible but barely credible events all.

We can see this trend most clearly in the virulent and ultimately self-defeating public debates that surround the issues of feminism, racism, and affirmative action today that spillover from college campuses to talk radio and Internet chat boardrooms. Looking dispassionately at the rhetoric that informs the issues exclusively, one sees that these debates have less to do with the real substance of the issues than a public brawl over who will control the way issues are presented and packaged to the public, whose McSlogan will be used to represent it. In this peculiar sense—in feminism's continuing definitional struggles, for instance—it's not the case of the issues that women have with each other and with men now as much as it is with the competing visions women have of themselves. This has ultimately turned feminism's focus into a debate over which advertising agency will be responsible for the campaign and whose artfully crafted photos and identifying captions will be hung over the cash register at the check-out line, in the boudoir, the office, or the voting booth. Soon enough the coded catch phrases take on a life of their own and individuals take a back seat to ideology, which pleases no one really.

Instead of specific knowledge—the antidote that would at least allow if not encourage reflection and informed action—we are swamped with undifferentiated sound bites the collection of which is substituted for informed understanding. And we accept the afterburn that accompanies it, that subtle intellectual indigestion that comes from having it "our way," day after day, and we've grown habituated to waking up hungry, ravenous for more.

Fast food is to food as bumper stickers are to political discourse, and one need not be a Ph.D. in political science or government to easily reduce any political campaign, be it for the presidency, state legislator, or school board, to its basic bottom line. It's clear that office seekers could just as well be selling hamburgers as representative democracy, since the pitches are so similar. Many contemporary and modern nuanced political scientists maintain that it's the price one pays for living in our democracy because people are so busy with their own lives that major issues must be reduced to idea McNuggets to be easily comprehensible and digested. They will further assert, when waxing poetic (usually before a national television audience or talk radio call-in shows), that in truth, the "business" of democracy is to provide a kind of consumer satisfaction, that representatives (senators, etc.) are in essence consumer advocate/ombudsman for its citizens; so using the junk food sell is a reasonable and justifiable approach.

151

Examining how various political programs from affirmative action to budget reform, from environmental conservation to gun control or even to the continuing evolution of the meaning of political correctness are packaged these days, we can see how harmful this is to us all. For cultural critics like Richard Schickel, the use of advertising techniques as a shorthand for informed understanding "ultimately destroys the capacity for subtler, more reflective, and therefore more dangerous confrontations with these issues, indeed with the infinite variety and complexity of our fellow human beings."[1] The "danger" comes in hearing out the other position and perhaps changing or modifying one's own views after one's mind has "been made up." Bigotry and racial stereotypes flourish in such an environment, where brand-name characterization is demanded for all ideas to be comprehensible. Consequently, and more to the point in Schickel's view, we also lose our capacity for abstract thinking and imagination, unless they too are neatly packaged.[2] (A similar criticism has been leveled at MTV and the other music video channels for what they have done to the imaginative component of music itself. In a rather major way, music videos limit the meanings of songs to one "authorized" image instead of allowing the mind to make its own visual connections, its own video that changes with the circumstances and environment; not that the target audience really seems to mind so much watching the radio.)

Of course, in 1837 Alexis de Tocqueville nailed it in *Democracy in America* by noting that one of the characteristic wrinkles of American democracy "is not that it leads men away from the pursuit of forbidden enjoyments, but that it absorbs them wholly in quest of *those which are allowed* [emphasis mine]."[3] Like Huizinga's descriptive characterization of America as a land of "This, Here, Soon," it's another covalent term for American junkfood consumerism, burgers and Cokes or tabloid journalism, a far more elegant and polite description of the illusion of having it your way when it's actually theirs.

When this tendency is translated into the mechanics of representative democracy, the purpose of a successful political campaign is to convince an electorate already habituated to instant gratification that they are having it "their way" when they vote for The Candidate, the political equivalent of the menu photoburger that gives us the heartburn later on. However, if the voters are already deciding on muddled homogenized sound bite burgers, the newly elected senator, congressman, assemblyman, etc., is far worse off in believing her or his bumper stickers when the realization hits that in truth the special interests to whom (s)he is beholden, who bankrolled their campaigns in reality have succeeded in having it "their" way—and to hell with the poor schmucks who don't have the money, the ordinary constituents. On the other hand, the incumbents, habituated to the system as it has evolved, already know the drill, grit their teeth, and try to get something done as best they can. Third-party and fourth-party alternatives that occasionally try to reform the system fail, because ultimately the electorate's fascination with and dependence on franchise-style politics is so overwhelming that they are forced into debasing while homogenizing whatever it is they thought they were standing for so everyone can be "for it." Or, on the other hand, as in the case of the recent third-party run by Ross Perot, where a need might be there but a quirky millionaire industrialist as candidate might not be really up to the rigors of the campaign, they bail out and leave supporters in the lurch and adrift with their discontent unfocused save for the vestigial "I Can Fix It" bumper sticker.

"If," in the words of the poet E. E. Cummings, "freedom is a breakfastfood," and that's how representative democracy is marketed, is it any wonder that Americans are suffering the fastfood "afterburn," that fewer people are even bothering to vote, or that modern presidents are elected by a little more than a quarter of the registered voters these days? Since the late sixties fast food political techniques have taken over the American electoral process, its methods having become so blatant and transparent that in the presidential election of 1992 between Bill Clinton and George Bush, voters were treated to the spectacle of partisan political managers being interviewed, immediately after the candidate's debate, by learned TV commentators who folded the respective partisan spins into their own "objective" assessments of the candidates' performance. It was almost like taking the word of the racetrack touts and posting the winners from their morning line instead of waiting until after the race was run or interviewing the owners in the *middle* of the race: "The horse has great heart, especially in the back stretch; all things being equal, the filly should win, etc."

This wasn't electoral politics, but PR personality marketing masquerading as news—just another manifestation of that glossy superburger picture over the cash register. In the nineties, the candidates and their campaign manager/handlers don't even bother to hide their strategies from the electorate; it's all out front. No wonder Americans are becoming resigned, distressed, and dispirited. Not only do they tell you what they're going to do and how they're going to do it (which issues, what spin, etc.), but amazingly enough, they go ahead and do it too. And they do it because we've become so depressed that ultimately we let them. Have it your way? Of course, you can. Would you like fries with that?

That's what I was thinking about when I reached the bottom of my eldest daughter's toy bin and extracted a miniature top-hatted Uncle Sam figure. Was that just another promotion for *Troy, New York*, a movie that had come and gone with fries and a shake? Or some sort of federal government promotion for the Fourth of July?

By now it was 3 AM and I was tired. Well, perhaps my daughter would tell me where it came from if I happened upon it again. At least I hoped so. On second thought, I pocketed it for my own collection.

Chapter 7

Asking Alice

Fighting for the Right to Party

Here's a riddle, actually a variation on an old studio musician's aphorism: Why is it that if you're working a folk gig, all you'll ever be able to score is pot? The crowd's always pretty mellow, looks like the normal bunch of sixties hippies. As long as it's mushrooms, you really can get anything you want from the same crowd at a Phish or Rat Dog concert. Same goes for cocaine, poppers, or downers at the disco, where the seventies style and the retro spirit of *Saturday Night Fever* inhabit those glitzy interiors like flies in amber. At the reggae/ska/dub clubs where the natty dreds hang, jah-filled spliffs abound, while at rap and gangsta concerts, urban and suburban wanna-be rappers love to toke on their blunts, hollowed-out cigars filled with marijuana. Nothing but uppers and beer in the biker-effect black leather, chain 'n' chrome heavy metal universe; Ecstacy, Vitamin K, or the designer drug of the moment is readily available in the "cutting-edge" rave scene where black-garbed industrial noise/techno folks meet to freak.

To the proverbial visitor from another planet, all this behavior seems so clannish, quaint, and tribal, this connection between each music scene and the drugs that go with it. How did these "mores" evolve? What were they to begin with, and in what ways over the past 30 years have they been transformed? How we answer these riddles not only says much about what we are as a nation so totally consumed and obsessed with pop culture but also helps to explain how we got to this point in the first place. There's a common thread running through this naturally: Unless one has chosen to willfully ignore the past 40 years of American social history, it comes as no shock to realize that not only a fair percentage of today's teenagers, unofficially put at more than 40%, but a larger if no longer as well-documented number of former teenagers, i.e., their parents, are now or have been intimately familiar with the meaning of Bob Dylan's song "Rainy Day Women #12 and 35." Granted, some of us no longer follow Mister Zimmermann as closely as we did, we may "not inhale" that much anymore, but just like the song says, "everybody must get stoned."

But we do, we have, four generations of us in one particular fashion. Perhaps "You Can't Always Get What You Want" by the Rolling Stones or "Trucking" or "Casey Jones" by the Grateful Dead will always raise a knowing crinkle of recognition in future teenage eyes, perhaps not. It's comforting nonetheless in this Post-Elvis Age to realize that many of us cohabit the same musical/experiential universe. Sex and drugs and rock and roll; rock and sex and drugs and roll, these are the familiar rites of initiation into contemporary American adolescence, even if it seems to last into early middle age now. Though the cultural contexts of these songs and newer ones have been substantially modified over time to fit new contexts by their commercial uses, they remain an integral part of our media musical consciousness. Pop music in all its hues, tastes, and varieties, from hip-hop to reggae, from a capella oldies to vintage psychedelia, is the hardest-working component of the material/commercial world of big business: its riffs, catchy hooks, and especially the inherent "attitude" accompany the strutting supermodel parade on the media catwalk before our eyes and ears. There's so much music product to choose from, so much seeming variety, yet paradoxically less and less *music* capable of stirring souls. It may appear that we are not even listening to the same music from the same pew, or as members of the same church for that matter. But though we may hearken to different preachers and sing different doxologies, still each of us is product of and worships at the church of rock and roll. Its images and attitudes inform our world.

Riddle me this: The Beatles, who broke up more than 25 years ago, were in 1996 enjoying their best album sales yet, having sold 6 million out of their own old catalogue and achieved a combined sales figure of almost 20 million for their recently released anthologies. That's astonishing enough given the complexity of the music business, but even more mind-boggling is that an estimated *41%* of those buyers were teenagers who weren't even born when the Beatles were first popular in the early sixties.[1] Listening to *Sgt. Pepper's Lonely Hearts Club Band* through a set of earphones or on a really expensive audio system while investigating and decoding its every musical detail and nuance, checking and noting every overdub, every cross-fade between channels, remains a compelling experience for many more generations now. Hearing for the first time that chair squeak at the end of the orchestra glissando, the conclusion of "A Day in the Life," remains a delicious discovery too. After all this time we're kidding ourselves if we refuse to admit that *Sgt. Pepper's* attention to detail, its textual continuity, is no longer (or never had been) amplified, enhanced, aided, and abetted by judicious applications of marijuana (or LSD or mushrooms, for that matter). That, in short, *Sgt. Pepper's* was created expressly for stoned people and continues to function as a meditational aid in that capacity is, in the words of the veritable Parson Weems, "too true to be doubted."

Likewise the music of Jimi Hendrix and the Doors continues to exert its intergenerational fascination. Perennial backlist mainstays for more than 25 years, the records of these artists annually produce royalties at the six-figure level for heirs and record companies alike.* That observation alone speaks well of the continued popularity and profitability of the "golden oldies" format on "Classic Rock" FM radio stations.

---

*According to a survey conducted by the *Oprah Winfrey Show* in 1996, Jim Morrison of the Doors was the seventh-richest *dead* rock star, with Elvis first and Jimi Hendrix fourth (there are statistics for everything, Virginia).

If we look beyond the tale of the commercial tapes for a moment, something less quantifiable but more concrete becomes apparent. These numbers document and underscore the growing hunger of new generations not only for the music of that "old time" space and place but also for the "spiritual" values those works embodied (which flip postmodernists denigrate and dismiss as "all that hippie bullshit"). Still, whether hidden within the subtexts of television commercials or mutated beyond belief by selective motion picture or video recreations, somehow those "old" values continue to induce younger generations to examine them in their pristine forms via CD or cassette and expropriate these essential texts for their own adolescent rites of initiation.

Considering America's present hypocritical ideology concerning drugs, it seems totally out of character that any kind of consciousness and lifestyle could be or ever was ever associated with music. For nineteenth-century American utilitarians, there were two sorts of drugs available: those that cured you (in short supply and virtually nonexistent) and those that doped you up while nature ran its course. The latter, avidly ingested for all sorts of ills, real and imagined, were widely available in large quantities from the patent medicine industry in potions that contained varying doses of opium and cannabis derivatives.

By the nineteenth-century, according to Dean Latimer and Jeff Goldberg's *Flowers in the Blood: The Story of Opium,* the drug trade was starting to be a major staple of American commerce. In 1840 there was so much opium being imported for "medicinal" uses, 24,000 pounds, that the United States Customs Office put a duty on it that raised the wholesale price to $1.40 a pound. Ten years later, 87,000 pounds were imported. By 1860, the price was $4.50 a pound and the United States was importing 105,000 pounds. By 1870, the amount clearing customs had more than quadrupled to 500,000 pounds, while the paid duty cost per pound had been raised to $2.50 per pound. This figure excluded the approximately 25,000 extra pounds that were being smuggled into the country by canny sea captains and traders.[2]

The drug industry grew explosively when opium was further definitively and cheaply refined into its 24 alkaloids. The most powerful and cheapest to produce was morphine,

> much cheaper than alcohol for the euphoric tickle it gave you, and every pharmacy and general store carried preparations of it calculated to appeal to every sort of person alive, whatever the individual emotional quirk or physical ailment. There were lower-proof opiates like laudanum or codeine, in tasty syrups and candies, to inculcate in novices of any age an appreciation of opium's particular extra-therapeutic properties, and to insidiously lead them, through a succession of higher-proof nostrums, to morphine itself.[3]

From corner drugstores or traveling snake oil salesmen, morphine was also readily available to the discerning consumer in tablet, ointment, solution, tincture, suspension, and clyster (enema) form. The mania for self-administered opiate medication in the mid-1880s was given a "boost" by the development, production, and widescale marketing of high-quality syringes and needles, while "the appearance of pure, cheap, cocaine hydrochloride was everywhere enthusiastically greeted, and sales of more traditional pharmaceutical highs like chloral hydrate, ether, and cannabis tinctures suddenly took off on a handsome surge."[4] The industry that serviced the "medicinal" demands for this epidemic of American nervousness grew by leaps and bounds, and opiate use in the United States grew at a rate considerably steeper than the general increase in the population.[5]

It may have been one thing for a nation of white Americans to self-medicate themselves into a stupor for imagined or real ills, accounting for the increased consumption by many people who never wound up being full-fledged addicts and documented as official statistics. From a peculiarly skewed point of view, however, America's mass underground addiction to codeine-laced cough syrup (among other concoctions) was a fitting symbol of nineteenth-century progress and civilization, mirroring and aping the social problems that England in the Victorian Era or France in La Belle Epoque had as social consequences of the trade, a worthy example of capitalism's ability to meet the demands of the market in the same way. Perhaps, too, this need for better living through industrial chemistry among the leading Western powers, this hallmark of a "modern" civilization, was an essential component of The White Man's Burden. Or even that addiction was an anthropomorphic indicator of a modern colonial nation's "masculinity"; that is, if one considers chemical dependence as an exclusively masculine trait. (This last notion, currently under revisionist attack, may no longer appear to be as true in our progressive age of politically correct thinking.)

162

Given all this, it may have been possible to condone such addictive excess in America among the dominant white population, but never for any nonwhite group, especially the Chinese and newly enfranchised African Americans. As the century drew to a close, it became an increasingly acceptable political tactic to demonize drug use among the Chinese and African Americans and color it with racial stereotypes that neatly deflected blame away from the ethics of the over-the-counter (or out-of-the-wagon) patent medicine industry that profited from it. The Chinese were attacked and ridiculed for their "devious foreign ways," though by their substantial contributions to America during the building of the transcontinental railroads in midcentury they were entitled to American citizenship if they so chose. To their credit, they successfully carved out a separate but coexistent society in large American cities like San Francisco, Chicago, New York, Philadelphia, and Boston, where their culture, crafts, and cuisine were widely available to be enjoyed by those who bothered to investigate them on their own. And yet one of the favored yellow journalist cartoon visions concerned the crafty and sinister opium-smoking Chinese white slaver leading "good" girls to disgrace, a characterization that seemed for a time to appeal to the redneck mother population in the agrarian hinterlands of America.

For native-born, newly enfranchised African Americans, the approach was far more insidious and twisted, because it was targeted against their unique music culture, despite the fact that minstrel and ragtime music was already thoroughly integrated into nineteenth-century American life. To the politicians who encouraged these racist sentiments as well as the newspaper editorialists who promoted them, African-American music was an insidious conveyor of racial impurity and cultural miscegenation, and African Americans were to be feared as "the other"— the designated emotional dark side of the American psyche. It was one thing to listen to this music, to even enjoy it, but not to acknowledge freely or openly the origins or give respect to the culture from which it came. Unless black ragtime and jazz (and, indirectly, the group that created it) were marginalized or limited to function within certain stereotypical parameters, if not suppressed altogether, one risked losing one's cultural identity as an official White Person in Anglo-Saxon America.

And so it was that the associated evils of race mixing that came from the volatile mixture of jazz and opiates circulated in the popular press before World War I along with lurid stories about African American "cocaine-o-mania"—a widely circulated folk myth that African Americans were the only people who had violent reactions to drug overdoses. Authors Latimer and Goldberg cited "Negro Cocaine 'Fiends' are a New South Menace," an article by Dr. Edward Huntington Williams that appeared in the *Sunday New York Times Magazine* in 1914, describing how cocaine turned black men into veritable werewolves:

> consumed by violent homicidal passions and, worst of all, invulnerable to bullets . . . with the story of a police chief in Ashville, North Carolina, who was called out to arrest a "hitherto inoffensive negro" who was "running amuck" in a cocaine frenzy: "Knowing that he must kill the man or be killed himself, the Chief drew his revolver, placed the muzzle over the Negro's heart, and fired—'intending to kill him right quick,' as the officer tells it. But the shot did not even stagger the man. And a

second shot that pierced the arm and entered the chest had just
as little effect in crippling the Negro or checking his attack.
Meanwhile the chief, out of the corner of his eye, saw infuriated
Negroes running toward the cabin from all directions. He had
only three cartridges remaining in his gun, and he might need
these in a minute to stop the mob. So he saved his ammunition
and finished the man with his club.[6]

A variation of these scare tactics was adapted by the Anti-
Saloon League and the Temperance Movements at the turn of
the century and used to sell the idea of Prohibition to the nation. The Volstead Act of 1919, banning alcohol sale and consumption in the United States from 1919 until its repeal in 1934,
proved to be an exercise in misguided altruism with unforeseen
consequences. Like the widespread indiscriminate use of opiates, there had always been a problem in America of defining
the line between social drinking and alcoholism. The choice to
imbibe and how was better left up to individuals or like-minded
individuals to decide, not the government, of course. Instead
of turning people away from alcohol, the so-called "Noble Experiment" elevated alcohol to the status of an illicit drug whose
consumption became an indicator of fashionable modernism.
In effect Prohibition *encouraged* people who never thought of
drinking or breaking the law to patronize speakeasies where
bootleg liquor was served. The generation of law-breakers Prohibition created facilitated the growth of a whole criminal un-
derclass to service the great thirst, much the same way patent
medicine manufacturers had leaped into the commercial
breach in the preceding decades. (Since the late 1960s, seven
presidential "wars" on drugs have apparently ignored or repressed knowledge of Prohibition's moral failure—if not the
consequences, its criminal hangover.) But maybe it was easier
to get people behind the idea of Prohibition, at least initially,
because it was an addictive drug with no cultural overtones attached.

Though they sold papers, inflamed mobs, and sometimes
even won elections, these racist campaigns hardly befitted the

sentiments of a nation sworn to defend Western civilization against the onslaught of the godless Huns in World War I, if indeed that was the purpose of the politicians and pamphleteers in the first place. In any case, the accomplishments of the Harlem Renaissance, that veritable flowering of black arts in the post-War twenties, definitively should have put paid to the notion of the inferiority of black culture. This especially held true for the "Flaming Youth" of the twenties who discovered this world on their own in the clubs and art galleries that grew up in Harlem and for those who discovered the energy of *le jazz hot* in Paris in the twenties.

From the twenties until the late forties, jazz in its various configurations, like rock and roll in our own time, was at one time deemed "countercultural" too. Whether performed live from radio studios or hotel ballrooms or played on records where black jazz was marketed and segregated as "race" music, it gradually became an integral part of America's musical pulse despite the fact that American society was functionally racially segregated. There were black jazz ensembles who played for predominantly black audiences as well as white "swing bands," like the Tommy Dorsey Band and the Glenn Miller Big Band, who translated the idiom while knocking off the more racy sexual innuendos for white tastes.

However, for the growing number of white jazz buffs who knew the difference, the Big Band Sound was a pale and hollow shuck-and-jive act compared to the authentic item. It wasn't until the midthirties, when Benny Goodman featured black players like Teddy Wilson and Lionel Hampton in his Trio and Quartet arrgegations and used arrangers like Fletcher Henderson and Don Redman in New York's Carnegie Hall Spirituals to Swing in 1938 and 1939, that the cultural barriers between white and black worlds began to crumble. Still, it wasn't until after World War II that integrated jazz bands were the norm and the inevitable mixing of cultures could no longer be ignored or officially marginalized.

This is where those artists, poets, musicians, and writers of the Beat Generation came on the scene and dived right into that rich musical, very American tradition. Enthusiastically they embraced be-bop, the counterstatement to the lush overorchestrated big band sound in the late forties and the "cool" school that grew out of it. By the early fifties archetypal Beats were mesmerized by players like Charlie Parker, John Coltrane, Eric Dolphy, Charlie Mingus, Horace Silver, and eternally Miles Davis, whose style projected their distance from the official "whiteness" of American culture. Beat poetry, those dense word-notes of cross-hatched blank verse chanted or scat-sung sometimes with jazz accompaniment, riffed off the hidden social history of black America, a mirror image of the cool, mournful, meditative, plaintive, intuitive, self-referential worlds the musicians inhabited. Reading Allen Ginsberg's incantory poem *Howl* or Lawrence Ferlinghetti's "The Dog" from *Coney Island of the Mind* or virtually any passage in Jack Kerouac's *On the Road*, originally conceived as one long literary jazz solo written on one continuous roll of paper, is a literary taste of the jazz universe the Beats inhabited.

By the late fifties and early sixties, the cool of jazz was folded into a heady cultural stew which was comprised of liberal doses of nineteenth-century American Transcendentalism (the poetics of Walt Whitman, Ralph Waldo Emerson sentiments) with an interest in Zen Buddhism brought on by American servicemen's contact with the Far East. Along with post–World War I French Surrealism, Dadaism, and post–World War II Existentialism, the resultant full-field intellectual overview proved to be irresistible for the next generation of college students. When further refined, the central metaphor came down to one goal: the search for consciousness, Self and Cosmic, the search for good maps. Everyone needs them; adolescents in any age need good maps when first becoming aware of the world at large, when beginning to ask questions not only about their ultimate place in the scheme of things, but *what it all means.* Knowing where to find the right kind of maps to get "The Rules" is crucial during that emotionally painful period of transformation in high school precisely because "the rules" are always changing. Consciousness of Self centered on the personal knowing and transformation that would put you in touch with who you were and what you could become, or so it was thought.

The correlative to Consciousness of Self, Cosmic Consciousness, was supposed to put one in touch and in synch with the larger universe and provide a set of invariant universal maps for behavior; even if they weren't aware of it at the time, the Beats provided for the next generation a set of roadmaps that seemed useful for the taking. In the long run, having the "right maps" in the Cosmic sense was far more useful than being dependent on mutable ones, those that adolescent peer group culture or the consumer society of the fifties were selling. When boiled down further, one's psychic survival revolved around being on The Path, The Way, and how you traveled was more important than the ultimate destination, which would take care of itself. (By the later sixties, the question was further distilled: "Are you on or off the bus?")

For the Beats there were two paths to enlightenment: In occult terms they were characterized as the Path of the Serpent and the Path of the Arrow. The Path of the Serpent was a slow, meandering, but seemingly inexorable journey that required intense contemplative study of many years by the seeker before the inner light was revealed. It was the way of monks, Zen masters, and ascetics like St. Augustine. A far more direct instantaneous approach (as well as a more social path) was the Path of the Arrow, which was entered by the use of drugs, be they caffeine and benzedrex ("benzedrine, the staff of life," was an old beatnik joke), marijuana, psilocybin mushrooms, or opium and its derivatives. Though the visions may have been ecstatic and intense, without the maps, metaphors, and "the knowledge," the Path of the Arrow produced a temporary result, a fleeting glimpse, an imitation of the meditational state.

On the other hand, sometimes a glimpse was all you could get (or all you really wanted or had time for), so the best that one could do under the circumstances was somehow to testify to that reality, to the possibility of attaining that vision, that feeling, and to attempt to translate that ecstacy into art, music, or poetry. Books like Allen Ginsberg's *Yage Letters* or Aldous Huxley's *Doors of Perception* and *Heaven and Hell* or the teachings of Timothy Leary in the latter sixties served as travelogues filled with field notes from these psychoactive excursions, and they conferred on the Path of the Arrow an aura of romance. Without the proper knowledge to take along on the Path of the Arrow, there was the temptation to become hooked on the various ways of "getting there" instead of staying and "being there," the supposed ultimate purpose of the whole exercise. The perverse visionary nightmare world of the psychically addicted in William Burroughs' *Naked Lunch* and *Nova Express* showed the darker aspects of the Path of the Arrow. For Burroughs, heroin was *the* working metaphor for the promise of consumer society as well as the ultimate commodity that consistently provided an ever-evolving, seductive, all-inclusive "reality"—a terminal addiction as any shop-a-holic maxed out on credit cards can attest. Burroughs' cautionary tales were also an integral component of the Beat legacy, and though bleak, were crucial if one was to fully comprehend the darker consequences of using drugs of transformation that amplified, mediated, and ultimately altered personal reality.

For one who chose to travel the Path of the Arrow, the stakes were high and the perils had to be addressed responsibly—Not for Everybody. To undertake this path for the wrong reasons, haphazardly on a dare without a patient and understanding guide, was the ultimate foolishness, cheapening and devaluing the psychic and spiritual initiation process. To experiment with psychoactive drugs essentially should have been an act built on faith and, above all, trust. It was the height of psychic folly to entrust the spiritual development of one's inner being to just anyone. The guide perforce had to be multifaceted and talented: a philosopher, therapist, priest, and DJ all rolled into one. The guide also had to have "been there" consciously enough to be able to share the experience, to be able to patiently answer whatever questions were raised during the course of the experience of the neophyte.

Once this knowledge was fully apprehended by the initiate and successfully demonstrated, in time it could be passed onward to yet another seeker, and so the tradition and the knowledge could be transmitted from mouth to ear to soul and back, from individual to individual. Such visions could take the form of a Mack Sennett movie directed by Federico Fellini (thanks, Jeff A.) or could be extrapolated by viewing the cycle of rebirth in a vase of cut wild flowers that withered and bloomed before one's eyes like a visual tape loop. The visions could and frequently did take the form of laughing the cosmic laugh for hours on end. Visions varied with individuals, as did the form of the lessons with which intuitive and competent guides were familiar. In the main, all such insights were variations built around learning about interrelated global psychic consciousness, eternity, human decency, personal responsibility, and the brotherhood of man—for want of a better word, Love, if only one had the grace to see it. And somehow, without these intuitions and revelations being written down anywhere, but rather orally passed onward and outward in this manner, these maps became part of a brief but living tradition.

From 1962 to 1966, the Paths of the Arrow and the Serpent commingled. Drugs with certain kinds of music made the heavenly spheres dance. It was here that the Beats connected with those who would eventually refer to themselves as Heads, who would themselves briefly integrate the knowledge from both paths and the traditions from which they sprung. To be even an apprentice Beat one had to be attuned to a larger worldwide cultural history. In music, that meant being familiar with the history and development of not only the jazz of Miles Davis, Charlie Mingus, and John Coltrane but also the music of J. S.

Bach, the rhythmic dissonances of Bela Bartok and Igor Stravinsky, Middle Eastern music, and American folk songs of Pete Seeger and the Weavers, and the blues of Josh White and Hudie Leadbetter, Ma Rainey and Bessie Smith. The music was to be found in coffeehouses and jazz clubs in the cities where musicians and poets came together, or on late-night jazz shows, or in books "borrowed" from older brothers and sisters who were reading the new poetry in college courses. Following the Beat Way for an apprentice high school Beat required effort, a personal statement, since examining the world from an intercultural as opposed to parochial viewpoint was a conscious act of subversion in the self-absorbed America of midcentury.

Once on this path, good sense and intuition led to other connections the material laid out; it was natural to investigate the poetry and art of William Blake and Walt Whitman, or William James' *Varieties of Religious Experience*, the cosmological theories of Carl Jung, the plays of Samuel Beckett. Why folk, jazz, and pot came together is anybody's guess; maybe it was just a natural organic connection, a potent alchemical mixture that brought the outlaws from mainstream American music and the culture it represented to each other in the end. Before the juggernaut of official commercial culture redirected the purpose of the trip, other forces were at work that also had a hand in defining what "the knowledge" was even as it floated out of the coffeehouse worlds on the McDougall Street–Los Angeles–Boston folk axis.

An equally opposite and far more "official" form of "counterculture" emanated from the parallel worlds of pop art in New York, Los Angeles, London, and Paris, one over which for a time Andy Warhol presided. Under his influence the timelessness of Cosmic Consciousness was transposed into the morally drained aesthetic universe of the Now, where Art and Celebrity were coequal. Ambition for fame and celebrity defined this world's moral parameters and gave it its edge, where Being There mattered less than Being *Seen* There. The Fame Game universe over which Warhol reigned was totally consumed by social and creative edge-walking and publicity. Hugh Kenner, the critic, described the high-culture variation of the Poetry edge as The Hack's Progress, or How to Make It in London with Poetry:

> By one version, you spend your first two years at Oxford getting known and published in the Oxford little mags. (Getting what published? Well, you know, some *poems:* little sensitive ways to say Lo, Lo or Shrug, Shrug.) In your third year you get your own little mag together, with as many names as you can bag, and launch it with a publisher's cocktail party in London. No second issue ever need appear. You are now ensconced on the carousel where the action is: round and round and round, you-review-me-I-review-you, and together we'll all see just who gets reviewed. This account, an ideal composite, is not alleged to fit anyone in particular; an especially hilarious variant is the story of X, who, alas, did it all and it didn't work. He ended up lecturing in the Farthest East, one version of the doom Waugh invented for Tony Last.[7]

171

The drugs needed for the pop art world, unlike the poetry world, either helped one maintain that psychic edge or acted as a pillow when one fell off or out of one's edge. In this high-gloss high-powered atmosphere of couture, museum openings, showbiz personalities, and international society, the only "folk" that mattered were the rich folk, and the only cosmic connections that meant anything were those that advanced careers, not the spiritual evolution of the soul. The high-stakes movers and shakers of machine-made culture took barbiturates to sleep, uppers to kick-start the morning, and alcohol to maintain the buzz until it was time to crash and then start the cycle all over again.* This was primarily a culture that thrived on extremes.

---

*During and into the late sixties when the pop art world was reigning supreme, there was a "Dr. Feelgood" practicing in New York whom the Beatles memorialized in their song "Dr. Robert." He was known for administering injections containing speed, vitamin B12, and multivitamins to celebrities and socialites alike, providing for a time (until he got busted by the local authorities) that one could speed one's brains out and still be healthy, rich, *and* thin.

The musical equivalent of urban edge in the pop art world, the virtual progeny of William Burroughs, was the Velvet Underground, who came out of Andy Warhol's Factory in the mid-sixties. The Velvets' shrieking, dissonant, brooding rhythms, when wrapped around lead vocalist Lou Reed's ironic lyric portraits and enveloped by John Cale's dark narcoleptic trance-inducing viola drones, portrayed a seamy seductive universe that romanticized the chrome-plated fashion nightmare in which the denizens of the high pop world existed. Instead of life-affirming and connection-making, the music of the Velvets reeked of sexual ambiguity, death-rush, psychic confusion, paranoia, and betrayal—the mirror image of the heroin edgeworld, which for those looking in from the outside of this kind of city life possessed a morbid fascination.

172

Whether by accident, design, or the fact that Fashion's needs are insatiable, in the eighties when the Velvets reemerged as a pop force, heroin use and addiction had been elevated to mythic status in the developing pop rock world. Over the last 30 years, for a legion of punk bands in Los Angeles and New York as well as any other urban center that aspired to host an artistic avant garde, heroin had come to be the drug of choice for those who craved the pretensions of *high pop* that the Velvets shilled for. Though undeniably dark, after 1967, this heroin lifestyle-aesthetic, the seeking of ever newer and sharper edges, became the operant mechanism that drove the music business through successive phases, and continues to this day in the world of rock and roll celebrity.

Unfortunately, the nature of this slow and gradual organic dissemination of "the knowledge," which had been taking place roughly in the period from 1962 to 1966, was irreparably altered and distorted by its electronic transformation during the so-called Summer of Love in 1967. Consciousness of the kind Heads sought never could be an easily accessible or readily manufactured mass commodity. Good guides had always been at a premium, in spite of what "straight" journalists, looking for a good catchy hook, advertised as they focused on the external trappings without bothering to burrow underneath. What was "discovered" and publicized was a series of easily comprehensible slogans, fashion pictorials, and store-bought goods: posters, faded jeans, tie-dye T-shirts, bongs, cigarette rolling machines, paisley wallpaper, "free" love, communes, the whole catastrophe. Promoted by *Time, Life, Look, Newsweek, Vogue, The New York Times,* and in time, *Rolling Stone,* "Head" consciousness became an irrelevancy; a separate reality was born. Anyone could look like they were "being there" (or had been there) without going through the discipline of the steps. Maybe it was inevitable, given the penchant of the American spirit to think of things in terms of commerce, that the knowledge itself was another failed Romantic effort to turn back the clock (or for that matter, to dispense with clocks entirely). What had been Not for Everybody in the early sixties by 1968 was for Anyone; the Nova Express had left the station.

By 1970 and thereafter, it no longer mattered that Heads eschewed alcohol and depressants or had pegged the oblivion express junkies were on for the baleful psychic influence it was bound to become. Heads were scorned as "elitists." Nor would it occur to the next generation for whom "the knowledge" was handily homogenized, commodified, and profitably distributed that Rock Culture, this new composite designer drug, would ultimately prove to be not only an inferior, but also a far more addictive, opiate than anything heads could have imagined.

Whole universes have been traversed since the fifties question "Can you hold your liquor" has become "Are you experienced?" while "listen(ing) to the color of your dream" seems to have gone out of fashion lately for those who choose the Path of the Arrow today. Fame, designer goods, technology's promise, or the pursuit of pleasure are today's drugs of choice; the culture of addiction that William Burroughs fluidly and eerily explored has been renamed "codependency," reduced to a staple topic for television talk shows. Here's progress for you:

While heroin's effects have been superseded by those of crack cocaine, whose ecstatic rush is far more extreme and of shorter duration, inevitably crack has become more cost-effective than heroin for the dealers who traffic in it, individuals and governments alike.

All products change, it's true; fashions in "illicit" drug use fluctuate, wax, and wane—as does the effectiveness of the over-the-counter and prescription varieties that medicate this society's ills. Enough time has passed so that we see the mechanism at work in popular media: *Miami Vice*, the wildly successful television show of the eighties that glamorized the high-stakes, high-edge underworld of the cocaine trade, spawned a thriving fashion subculture that glamorized not only the drug, but also the fashion attitude and music that accompanied it. Ironically, this show was popular during the height of President Ronald Reagan's much-publicized war on the South American cocaine cartels, the ultimate result of which was to bring down the price of cocaine sold on the street to a more affordable level for larger numbers of people, hard-core addicts and the curious alike. The old folk song maxim inherent in the lyrics, "Cocaine's for horses, not for men,/they say it will kill me, but they won't say when" has been definitively transformed into "Champagne don't make me crazy, cocaine don't make me lazy/ain't nobody's business but my own." But again, how can good maps be created when the moral and ethical landscape in which they should guide no longer has any solid foundations or a sense of its own living history? Still, the need for valid and meaningful adolescent initiations remains constant though its forms continue changing over time, as do the lessons they are supposed to uncover and disclose about society.

Music no longer possesses that spiritual/ideological connection; it's all a series of metaphors to mix and match while the Paths of the Serpent and the Arrow have been reduced to a Stairmaster in the living room that goes nowhere in particular but helps pass the time and keeps us in "shape" for the race.

Here's what remains of the "knowledge" from that time: David Bowie in all his incarnations continues to inspire the fashionably correct, and if he's just too strange, there's always the midnight screening for *The Rocky Horror Picture Show*, which accomplishes the same ends. We also know that the stoner kids (the apprentice pothead and hippies) are captivated by Phish or the Grateful Dead; the apprentice macho-men or self-styled bad-girls (what used to be considered the "greaser and hood" element in the fifties) check into the regalia-laden feudal world of heavy metal. Rap's and hip-hop's appeal crosses race and class lines to the point where the lyrical and visual conventions have been enthusiastically assimilated by mainstream commercial culture—which meets and matches in the celebrity realms of pro basketball and football. The offspring of the Velvet Underground take to the techno-clubs and grunge parlors equipped with the correct clothing and attitude or flattened-affect. We know we're in the country and western world when we hear on the jukebox "She's acting single, I'm drinking doubles." The nutritionally and psychically correct New Age devotees prize their own trance induction and channeling music. (Is Prozac the psycho-musical equivalent of Muzak in elevators and malls?)

We all know the drill by now, having gone through the changes ourselves. Each generation salvages what artifacts remain from the last, then adds its own little twist to the hippie/punk/new wave/grunge variations. We don't complain, don't ask why, don't even blink, though perhaps we sometimes grit our teeth in frustration. For some reason, we also don't tell the new kids about our own experience, how we've "been there, done that," not as much because they won't listen but because they're convinced that the light only shines for them. Eventually they'll figure that one out, but not soon enough to break the cycle.

What alcohol did for earlier generations of adolescents, music and drugs do now. Whether we choose to avail ourselves of the knowledge their use and abuse provided (and continues to provide now), the ultimate questions revolve around not only how we initially came to our knowledge, but also the quality of our adolescent initiation rites—if not the skill of our guides. The manner in which the Beat/Head initiations of the fifties have been debased in the nineties is a case in point. Twenty-five or 30 years is a long enough span of time in which to examine the consequences of allowing these singular initiations to become, in effect, items of commerce.

In any case, even if the knowledge of those old maps is willfully repressed, discarded, or just neatly stored away in a dusty attic trunk in the Memory Palace, rest assured, the news and electronic fashion media will give us their version of the knowledge music formerly provided and will keep us abreast of the newest fashions in consciousness. We'll always know when heroin has again become chic among the art set or what's the right designer outfit to wear or designer drug to use on the techno/industrial noise club scene, but we'll never know why. That our media provides the wrong answers to the wrong questions seems to be a moot point in our world today. That's the sorrow and the pity of this continuing party, because it *should* deeply matter to us all.

Chapter 8

Don't Touch Me There
Whatever Happened to Foreplay?

Forty years on, rock and roll continues to claim to be about sex. It hasn't been about foreplay for a long while, a concept damn near dead in the nineties, and one wonders not only who killed it but when. Where can one find "make out" music these days? Not on MTV or VH-1, unless condom manufacturers are sponsoring the music buzz clip. On the other hand, there's an awful lot of jingle music to have sex to; pop and rock music accompany almost every form of sexual behavior imaginable, from heavy metal bondage/domination sex to disco sex (pass the poppers, please). The video gangsta-rap variation technically isn't about sex at all, but rather violence, where women are portrayed as willing victims. And when women are the rappers, the men become the beefcake objects of desire attired in their $700 sneakers, club jackets, and gold chains. At the opposite extreme is New Age music sex (or is it sex music?), which is ethereal, nonviolent, and androgenous, without a bottom or backbeat to it. And where's the fun in that?

Admittedly, all this talk seems rather quaint in a decade where children are having sex at younger and younger ages, when the average 8-year-old knows more about it than most 20-somethings a few decades ago, where teenage pregnancies in this most civilized of nations continue to be the meat and potatoes of political rhetoric and a social worker's nightmare. For all the music that's out there to accompany sexual activity, very little of it really seems to concern itself with the needs of foreplay or, for that matter, with the essence of sexual activity itself.

Foreplay was what adolescents of both sexes in the fifties
practiced at slow dances to the accompaniment of "Teen Angel"
heard over the tinny speakers of cheesy .45 record players or as
they dry-humped in the back seats of their parent's cars at drive-
in movies or in remote Lover's Lanes while watching the submarine races. Maybe foreplay would (or could) eventually lead
to sex, and down the road to making love. Making love happened when two people who'd gotten over the surprise of
having sex for the first time had actually discovered how to
enjoy each other—but that's Foreplay 305 and we're still trying
to deal with the concept of Foreplay 101 and 102. Foreplay (actually petting) was all there was for adolescents, an end unto itself. Within its confines, rules, and rituals, boys were allowed to
turn into men and girls into women, and romantic love was always a possibility. It's not that way now; no one is supposed to
be tentative, and either one has the mechanics down or one
doesn't. He shoots, he Scores!! and there's no room whatsoever
for the indeterminacies of the relationships between the sexes in
the Post-Elvis Age. That's the problem with this brave new (old)
age. "Foreplay? What's that?" I'm not advocating bringing back
the fifties, God knows, but there were certain useful rituals back
then that were helpful for easing one "into it," that primordial
and timeless man/woman thing.

For boys trying to be men back then, inevitably the whole
of male/female relations revolved around "making out," which
for guys before MTV dealt with baseball imagery as a working
metaphor. Before hitting a "home run" became the norm, adolescent males contented themselves with "running the base
paths." Making out was an art, hence the term "make-out artist,"
and, in many ways, when raised to the level of art, was a more
exciting process than "making it"—if only because it lasted
longer. That one could only find out after one had been
"making out" for a while, but who really knew from that back
then? Not men, and only a few women at least until the early
seventies. Making out was so delicious precisely *because* each
person was under a certain amount of restraint. Which was

maddening for an adolescent because one logically didn't know where to go after getting all hot and bothered, all that blood pounding in your ears and you're fumbling about, frantically grinding away to "Teen Angel." There's no real room for stuff like that in the middle of a mosh pit, that kind of tentative, intimate touching; but then again, that's not the function of moshing for the predominance of men who do or the ladies who love them. Gotta have glove, I suppose.

"Making it" and "making out" were worlds removed for men; "making it" was a finite destination, a 3-minute can-you-dance-to-it kind of thing, all very digital, an act with neither mystery or ritual attached. "Making out," on the other hand, was very analog in nature, and that came with the ritual that preceded it: the ritual grope at the movies or in the back seats of cars. And the music of that time was music to fumble to while contemplating and trying to deal with *the rules.* Here in an age when there are virtually no rules, limits, or rituals, having rules took on, in retrospect, an erotic content. In more innocent times, those rituals involved heavy petting and dealing with many layers of clothing, removing the ceremonial panty girdle (which gives away how old the ritual really is). Maybe clothing was the key to the eternal female mystery, the labyrinth of the Great Mother.

181

Suffice it to say, adolescent foreplay revolved around un-informed gradualism. Guys never went from meeting somebody even to kissing without going through the appropriate rituals. Whatever you "got" was significant: a first date peck on the cheek, even a handshake would do for speculation's sake for "the time being." Which seemed an eternity in high school on Monday, when you wanted to know who you'd be with on Friday or Saturday night. Men/boys extrapolated what women/girls wanted from their "field research"; in retrospect a laughable concept consisting of hurried and/or wildly inaccurate conferences with friends about getting to "second base," what happened when caught stealing third (that situation where a girl would let you french kiss her but you couldn't get her bra off while doing so). Rituals, those little rules!, the mechanics and intricacies of female impedimenta! Those little hooks were difficult for clumsy lust-crazed fingers turning thumbs to dislodge in the heat of the moment. Definitely it was uncool to rip these contraptions off, traumatizing your date and yourself in the process—with the whole of the second balcony looking on.

True, by the early seventies, some women decided no longer to wear bras—as a political statement, mind; something was gained, undeniably and momentarily, but something was also lost in the foreplay area. (These days, though, it appears that undergarments are back in vogue, at least if we can extrapolate from the number of Victoria's Secret, Frederick's of Hollywood, and trashy lingerie stores there seem to be springing up in local malls throughout the country.) So getting the bra off was part of that ritual, but girls had to let you take it off, or at least help when the confident hand slipped to hopeless fumbling. During these strained eternities, when locked into an emotional hyperspace, no one spoke: Thoughts reverberated, check lists were consulted as one's well-programmed but maxed-out emotional computers scanned data banks weighing experience against past research. There was something to be said for research nonetheless.

But back in that early rock and roll time, the largest part of foreplay was spent learning about kissing and slow dancing, the most fun to learn, especially at parties where everyone else was more or less doing the same thing with varying degrees of success. You had to wait until a ladies' choice or a spotlight dance, or any slow dance and then *ask her*, the culmination of yet another set of foreplay rules fraught with a different set of variables. But say one got over that hurdle, in theory with a slow dance, one could be allowed (and maybe even encouraged) to practice and refine those techniques however they were acquired. To be honest and perfectly clear here, guys back then never really knew what girls were thinking. (For that matter, guys today *still* don't, only they project their 'tude better about it all. At the same time, the only reason men might know anything is that women are more vocal, but that doesn't mean that men know what women are *thinking*—they might think they do now, but they don't.) In the land of foreplay, thinking didn't take place on the level of language, but rather in the joint wordless, tactile exploration of a shared netherworld of moist silences, kissing, and slow dancing.

I was lucky back then to find a girl who liked me well enough to talk about the whole business to show me how to slow dance because I was such a cluck at it. Especially the technique of how to use my hands to deliberately (if apparently innocently) roam the female back to allow "the energy" build-up. This and more she showed me as we slow-danced in her rec room when her mother was out shopping one afternoon. (Not only was she a good dancer but also a *great* kisser.) The varieties of kissing! The open-mouthed kiss, the clenched-teeth kiss, and the variations in between. You knew you were striking out when you hit clenched teeth instead of moist lips. Sometimes you kissed off center then had to sort of work your way around. First kisses on first dates (assuming you had the opportunity) were problematic, especially that lead-in, which always seemed to be on the order of "ah . . . goodnight," and you'd steal a quick one before vanishing into the night . . . if she let you, for sometimes it took a few dates before she would. There were all these other steps and stages to go before "the deed" could have some meaning. Maybe I'd find out in college.

183

True, in the evenings from 7:30 to 11:30, the college library assumed an air of academic eroticism, where footsies under the table was the fore-foreplay to passing notes, to coffee dates, etc., etc., etc. More pitfalls. And if you really were crazy and obsessed with minute movements, you could very well wind up playing footsies with a chair leg. Which was embarrassing, but only to you. Then there were "study dates," which expanded how you dealt with women in terms of ritual. In college, girls were still girls, in the sense that the big wet silence still existed.

Late sixties psychedelic and early seventies art rock, even if now considered by some revisionists to be culturally incorrect, was a boon to foreplay, far more useful for rec room fumbling than those well-tempered slick Brill Building ditties back in the fifties. This was especially true for those long instrumental jams like the Chambers Brothers' anthem "Time (Has Come)." Significant others (though the list can be exhaustive as well as highly idiosyncratic) included, of course, the Rolling Stones' "Goin' Home" from their classic midsixties' album *Aftermath*, Marvin Gaye's "Sexual Healing" and "What's Goin On," and of course Led Zeppelin's "Stairway to Heaven," a world-class bit of make-out music if ever there was one. But while foreplay was given a larger musical context in which to "work" as an environmental aid for seduction (or whatever was passing for it), the Age of Liberation and Aquarius dawned, bringing with it an ideology intent on doing away with all forms of inhibiting sexual rituals. Along with sexism and male chauvinism in all its forms, foreplay, like God around the same time, was officially declared dead, or if not dead, then null and void. Damn, I'd just spent all those years perfecting my technique!

To be honest, the idea of "loving the one you're with," sappy as it sounds to youth today, when coupled with a wider use of the Pill, almost made foreplay an afterthought. There was lots of *talk* about sex, which everyone claimed to be having however they chose to have it. Everything was allowed: straight, gay, swinging, any kind of sex as long as it didn't cause a murder. It came down to "our bodies, ourselves," however "body" was defined. The neoscientific age was born; the messy age of hormonal humanism was officially in eclipse. Along with the new paradigms for sexual behavior came an inordinate amount of discussion about sexism in rock music among the females who'd formerly been the objects of lust and/or veneration, love or repulsion, but really (as always) approach and avoidance among the men. It was no big secret that the Rolling Stones had made a brilliant career out of their misogyny, as did lots of other groups; good rockin' for some, but where was the line going to be drawn between good old-fashioned rock and roll and new-fashioned ideological correctness? And exactly who was going to draw the line? Manuals abounded to herald the new age, for it was assumed not only that people had forgotten how to make love, but also to whom. (*How to Prolong Climax, How to Make Foreplay, The Joy of Straight Sex, The Joys of Gay Sex, The Consumer's Guide to Self-Abuse, The Harried Guide to Swinging,* or even *The Militant Feminist's Guide to Doctrinally Pure Sex* were never really written, but they might well have been, merely to get around the unscientific and uncomfortable predispositions of foreplay.) If all that doesn't kill foreplay dead, nothing can!

Though foreplay was officially and insistently declared dead by those in the know, vast numbers of people in the hinterlands still hadn't gotten the message. In the Aquarian Age, sex was again or still a commodity, and in terms of consumer satisfaction, no different than a color TV, a new car, a home computer. As with any other consumer product, sex, unlike foreplay, predicated on the expectation that what you put in you should be able to get out (with exception of some women and men who, once you put it in or it was put in to you, you'll never get it out, but this isn't an essay about bondage and domination, a discussion that can be left to the structuralists and deconstructionists in the audience). Maybe we had rock and roll to blame for all of this (and many did blame it), or perhaps that shows how materialism enervates the soul, as de Tocqueville has said elsewhere in this book.[1] That's what happens when there's too much official information. One wonders what he would have written about American adolescents today.

In the late sixties and middle seventies, though, sex, drugs, and rock and roll took the place of foreplay. In retrospect, this may have been the result of a male fantasy that drugs made sex

185

better, presupposing that men and women functioned in the same ways on the same drugs. Back in the Age of Psychedelia, it was assumed that if you dropped acid or mescaline with someone you loved, at least there was a kind of spiritual altruism at play, an emotional/mystical wish that surely it was possible to share an instinctual universe provided both people "peaked" at the same time. Not the case at all, and on further examination, not really such a transcendent psychedelic truth either, since, for the most part, women didn't need psychedelics as they functioned on another level entirely. It is equally true in retrospect that this idea may have been predicated on an essentially male version of the way women's psyches worked, and furthermore, it was *the men* who needed the drugs to break down their own emotional doors of perception. And even if this notion was misguided, it beat the hell out of sex divorced from any sort of emotional involvement at all. Most women were already definitely A-1 out there, thank you very much, Mr. Owsley. Give a woman a hit of Orange Sunshine and you'd never be able to catch up.

Did New Age sex come without foreplay? Was it "Love me, love my dogma?" Yes, because the doctrine that supplanted muzzy sixties emotional altruism was disco, a form of music and a social ideology antithetical to the concept of foreplay. Instead of having relationships, one "partied" at the disco, where one had sex in an industrially controlled environment. And not even on the dance floor, but in the toilet (somehow fitting, that). There was no reason to go to the toilet at the disco save to get loaded or have sex, or both. *Everyone* knew that you "went" before you came (depending on your sexual preference, of course). You didn't even have to take your clothes off for disco sex; that was reduced to a kind of impersonal sexual shorthand of fellatio, the blow-job favored by straight and gay men, though this depended on the class of disco one frequented. A snort of Peruvian marching powder, a quick blow-job, was an act of sexual consumerism that required little emotional commitment and absolutely no foreplay. There was a certain high school

aura to doin' it in the bathroom, much like smoking in the boys'
or girls' room in high school for earlier ages—times change not
much. The disco world was all about the moment. People didn't
go to discos to find love but to get laid. Oh, you went to psychedelic dances or peace rallies in the sixties to get laid too, but
usually you went somewhere else to do that—your place or
mine.

If the late sixties was all about making love and foreplay,
the seventies was all about having sex. The sixties may have
been about liberation, but the seventies was about license—that
you could do whatever you wanted to do with whoever you
wanted to do it, and that was all right. One's sexuality was a
matter of personal choice, and a fashion statement too. In
short, the seventies had brought out the swinging singles mentality, which proposed object love: You made love to someone
to prove that you could, not because you enjoyed it. Who knew
or cared what women wanted? Who cared what anybody
wanted for that matter; a therapy would present itself later on,
along with better drugs to dull the pain of concept sex. The age
of glam rock and disco sure may have appeared to be a wonderful whirl of fashion, but to adolescents just coming into their
own sexual knowledge it merely confused matters more precisely because there were no rules, there was no emotional ante-
room, no foreplay.

187

It did appear, to me at least, that the "New Age" feminism
of the late sixties that rose to meet the challenges of liberation
and whose effects are still being debated a quarter century later
initially robbed women of their singularity. Perhaps this loss of
individuality was useful from a doctrinaire point of view, but
from the idea of old-fashioned romance, it was totally mis-
leading and nonproductive. Doctrinaire feminism substituted a
joyless, humorless, spiritual materialism for sensuality. Wasn't
foreplay a humanist rather than a feminist or an economic
issue? So now it was okay for women to pleasure themselves but
no longer for men to pleasure women—what was happening?

For the conscious men in this heady age of self-knowledge and liberation, foreplay with newly entitled feminists at best was a chancy proposition, more uncomfortable than any fumbling they'd done at the submarine races a decade or so before. Whatever a man did or didn't say, do or didn't do, was scrutinized according to the latest ironclad ukases on sexism. And if one wasn't particularly a male chauvinist at the beginning of the evening, there was the possibility of becoming a raving one at the end just for spite. The result was that men became even more confused, since they were still enamored of the mysticism, magic, and romance they thought women personified. Men had been trying to solve the riddle of women for aeons, even if sometimes the results proved fatal, as Eric Newman remarked in his seminal study *The Great Mother* when he noted that "the numerous princesses who present riddles to be solved do indeed kill their unsuccessful suitors. But they do so only in order to give themselves willingly to the victor, whose superiority, shown by his solving of the riddle, redeems the princess herself, who *is* the riddle"[2] At last there weren't going to be any more riddles for men to solve. Who needed women to personify them? To become them? To pose them? But what was happening to the vital connection between men and women in the process?

Did feminists want to bore all men to death with no mystery or ritual? Apparently, but *like*-mindedness was just as constricting and ultimately frustrating as *no*-mindedness. Apparently those men who were drawn to the mystery of women were on to something that women possessed and had presided over for aeons. Mystery was always the biggest selling point of full womanhood, even with the great Female Acid archetype. Meanwhile, there were plenty of arguments surfacing that definitively proved that foreplay was an invidious form of sexually exploitative male behavior, though exactly who was exploiting whom was never really satisfactorily spelled out. For a time the message was who needed men anyway—sisterhood was beautiful provided everyone read from the same press release. Foreplay was either 20 minutes of begging and pleading or a total hype.

When foreplay was declared dead and then reinvented as a form of socialist sexual egalitarianism, female individuality was sacrificed. Unfortunately, these new authoritarians overlooked the fact that instead of rules, women just needed encouragement. Inevitably, feminist rhetoric expanded into the same dismal and ultimately dumb rhetorical and totalitarian spaces into which leftist male politics had sunk long ago. And how much finger-pointing or guilt-tripping could men endure before a reaction set in? Foreplay, who cares, we don't even have an arena in which to establish a dialogue, said the men who also wanted to evolve. Happily these days, an increasing percentage of women are starting to realize that their "official" stereotypes were just as chauvinist and humanly counterproductive and that men *and* women seek singular satisfactions: hugs, rubs, and companionship. If sex was merely a specific object-oriented consumer good, then sex itself was a barren and soul-enervating exercise.

For all the talk about feminism in the late sixties and early seventies, ironically about the only place where any progress was being made in terms of equality was within the field of rock and roll. Though in some ways hidden under the rubric of "publicity assistant" or "management assistant," women exercised considerable influence. In bands, either women were back-up singers or fronts, rarely musicians on their own. However, it was in the field of rock journalism, formerly a closed shop, where women came into their own. These early pioneers were in a class by themselves, and woe to the man—or for that matter the group—who told them differently! Without benefit of doctrine, unique creations all, these ambitious and fearsomely intelligent women gave as good as they got, to overcome the goddess/groupies stereotype. To be taken seriously by not only their male colleagues but also by the musicians themselves, they had to beat the men at their own sexist game because like it or not, rock and

roll had always been a boy's club. These literary ladies could and
frequently did out-smoke, out-drink, and sometimes even out-
fuck their male counterparts. Some musicians mistakenly
thought that if they managed to bed the lady journalist, they'd
be assured good reviews. Nothing particularly novel in that
thought; some things never change in profile tabloid journalism.
Though a lead singer (or lead guitarist or drummer) might or
might not be able to perform in the sack, if he failed to deliver
on stage, a negative review was the rule, not the exception; so
whatever temporary marginal utility performers thought they
were gaining over the journalistic process evaporated in a New
York minute. Men were men, women were women; but art was
art, which most of these rock and roll women journalists never
thought of confusing with publicity—something their male
counterparts had a habit of doing all the time.

It might appear that the rules have changed in the nineties,
but no one has apparently been successful in convincing generations of adolescent males of the fact. They still insist on the
same male fantasies that certain forms of rock and roll continue
to provide, regardless of what media feminists would like to
think. What continues to be offered at least visually and lyrically
is the same old product: sex without the courtship ritual attached—which is what foreplay was supposed to provide.
Modern entertainers like Madonna play by those old rules,
while academic feminists fail to realize that she's not an avatar
or creature of their ideology but purely of show business's. And
as for the music video sex that bundles her public image, that
seems to be just too product- and image-specific to be of much
use save as a "self-help" aid. After a while it's all too much of a
set piece, the imagery too standardized to allow any room for
foreplay, which deals with uncertainties and shades of meaning.

Enough already with chromium motorcycle sluts of various genders in bondage leathers, boots, and garter belts ca-
vorting in pseudo-Gothic dungeons or after-hours clubs or
homeboys in their Beamers airing out their bitches in the 'hood.

That's not even sex, it's power whose visions have been approved by the OPA (Orgasmic Protection Agency). In music video sex-land there's no room for representations of silences, hugs, and rubs anymore, just more polemics and more manuals for accessing the industrial commodity, not to mention more psychiatrists who specialize in sexual dysfunctions, more naked paper women, more MTV cybersex, more phone sex. No room for rituals here save of the industrial kind.

Though it is said that pop music is about romance while rock and roll is about sex, neither seems to address the issue that women, plain and simple, want to be appreciated for themselves, not held up against a chauvinist checklist of predigested specifications. It appears that women need to be treated with the respect due their position as the other half of the divine equation, so that in sex and in love a third more powerful entity evolves—that state that emerges when, in the middle of lovemaking, time ceases to exist and a delicious deep wet blackness descends, the kind of experience that reduces partners to a state of astonishment, the "what-was-that?" experience. There's no liberation in the rock and roll music world if sex is reduced to one specific vision or a series of specific visions.

191

Many years ago *Esquire* magazine published a survey about the perfect woman. No one was surprised that the respondent males wanted someone to take care of the kids, to look presentable, to entertain, do the chores, balance the books, clean up the kiddie poo, pick up the laundry . . . in short, a wife. Everyone wants one of those, including most women, and why not? That men appear to want a slave, not an ally, shows how frightened they are of themselves, how imprisoned they've become by their own roles that media feminism has foisted upon them. It's also a little sad to think that men want their lives transformed by the *service* not the *love* of a good woman, that men prefer to be maintained in their weakness. And, of course, most men don't understand that male chauvinism is an outmoded industrial concept that is not only psychically damaging but also financially ruinous, especially these days. In truth, women lose their natural transformatory powers by assuming the roles that doctrinaire feminists would like them to play, by ignoring the fact that good sex takes place among equals, not those habituated to roles. Is it any wonder that newsstands are glutted with pictures of buttered buns and air-brushed breasts on MTV vision of women? Whores or goddesses or just regular gals. Still, selling women using men's rules to do it is how music works in the nineties, like it or not.

People need more mystery and less science and industry. When a large industrial power is totally involved with sex as an industrial commodity, where is pleasure? If the object of all this technology is to make what is natural into a commodity, people would be better off in politics. It's really the politician's delusion that sex for money is somehow better than freely given sex, but considering what most politicians want a hooker to do to them, is it any wonder they have to pay for it? Everyone knows that working girls never get their due. But if they weren't doing their jobs, we'd all probably have a lot more wars so that politicians could watch. It must be a sign of status to be able to pay for sex, but I guess paying for it somehow makes it seem all right. Militant feminists have been saying so for a decade or more, what's to disagree?

So while sex has become inextricably tied to politics, romance remains an uncomfortable emotional issue—along with the difficulty of separating love and romance from politics. Rock and roll has always skated on thin ice here; it used to be about foreplay and courtship, but we no longer have any time for those things. If one makes love with the idea of making a political statement, as it seems people have doing lately, then the end result will be unsatisfactory: concept love, gimme some of that concept love. Concept love really doesn't keep you warm at night. If lovers started off as friends first, they'd still have something after the love gave out; any relationship that doesn't have friendship as its basis is doomed to failure anyway.

The big lie that pop and rock music continue to promote is that most men are convinced that friendship is impossible with women and that the only way to deal with them is as objects to be manipulated, used (and therefore abused). In truth good friends don't play those kinds of games. If men started off having friendship instead of sexual mastery at the root of their interactions with the opposite sex, they'd be far happier with the results, because friendship can lead to the intelligent man, and evolution takes place.

Getting "the woman's point of view" is always helpful when navigating through, getting over, or even starting a love affair. By talking *with*, not *at*, women, one learns about other women and how they perceive men. One learns how to see with the heart instead of the eyes too. And it's amazing just how many women feel limited by the physical body, why they're all so naturally drawn toward the occult. "Gee, I didn't know she had a brain," say men who've evolved to the next level of awareness. Men need to understand that it's just as devastating to be related to by a woman as a hunk with balls. Our bodies, ourselves? Hardly.

It's a shame that Americans have forgotten how useful rituals were for getting to know someone, for breaking the ice, for easing the tensions that allowed nascent feelings to blossom. At the same time, this emphasis on the marginal utility of foreplay has paradoxically lead to increased frigidity and fear; one doesn't tune the string of the violin unless one is prepared to play the tune. How humane and enlightened can a society be if it abolishes foreplay in the name of progress or leaves it to psychiatrists, magazines, sexual politicians, or even rock and roll music, when it makes much more sense to return to simpler pleasures and sensations, to re-create the feeling of that first tentative kiss wherever or whenever it was, no matter how embarrassed one might have been.

Chapter **9**

White Punks on Dope
Why Camille Paglia Is Academe's Answer to Betty Page

I too think the intellectual should constantly disturb, should bear witness to the misery of the world, should be provocative by being independent, should rebel against all hidden and open pressure and manipulations, should be the chief doubter of systems, of power, and its incantations, should be witness to their mendacity. For this reason, an intellectual cannot fit into any role that may be assigned to him . . . An intellectual essentially doesn't fit into any pigeonhole completely.

V. Havel[1]

A new generation is coming on the scene. . . . They won't use your knowledge and they will call you "sick" and "way-out" and that will be a sad day, but we must be prepared for it. For on that day they will have abandoned the other world they came here with and will become mundanists, pragmatists and concretists. They will shout loudly about soul because they will have lost it. And their protests will be a shriek, A manic sound. That's just the way it goes, brothers.

Ishmael Reed[2]

When *Mumbo Jumbo*, Ishmael Reed's satiric novel about the twenties' Harlem Renaissance and black and white history appeared in 1972, it was hailed for its fantastical free-wheeling take on American culture. Within the context of those truly psychedelic multicultural times of late sixties and early seventies, the novel was a perfect prism for examining black history, with its sharp-focus sidebars and divagations on his favorite areas of interest: Egyptology and the Osiris myths, voodoo, jazz and the birth of the blues, Masonic conspiracies, ofay hipsters and hepcats, left- and right-hand path magic and mysticism, plus of course (and always underneath as the beat) the struggle of good and evil, themes he still explores today. Though a book of its time, nevertheless, it was timeless in its cultural sweep and in its evocation of the living spirit of American history, segregated as well as integrated, a present with a presence of the past and using the twenties in Harlem to take a snapshot of America *in media res.*

It's not an anachronistic stretch even now to imagine Abdul's diatribe to Papa LaBas (see Ishmal Reed's epigraph above) coming from any of the participants in the debate over multiculturalism or any number of other evanescent intellectual flavor-of-the-month debates raging today. Reed took no prisoners then, figuring no doubt that he'd covered the subject, but almost a quarter-century later he has returned to the debate with *Japanese by Spring*, a picaresque novel of academia about the illuminating journey of a black professor, Charles "Chappy" Puttbutt, in his pursuit of tenure. Existing uneasily in the interdisciplinary metaspace between the departments of English and

African studies, Puttbutt has managed to keep himself as inoffensively aloof as possible while walking the ideological tightrope, much to the annoyance of his erstwhile colleagues who are always in need of allies in their interdepartmental struggles. In the turbulent atmosphere of Oakland University, though the good professor by dint of continually re-creating and reinventing himself has dodged many bullets and is now up for tenure, the forces of contradictory ideologies are conspiring against him.

By happy accident, while studying Japanese to improve his job prospects in case he *is* canned, Puttbutt is taken under the wing of his language instructor, actually the frontman for a Japanese business consortium with designs on his university (cultural conspiracies are nothing new within Reed's cosmology). Because of Chappy's eminent ideological pliability as departmental outsider, when the coup goes down, he becomes his mentor's chief administrative assistant. Instead of the ass kisser, he becomes the kissee in charge of promotion as well as the arbiter of future departmental agendas. Faced with all this power after being the interdepartmental *shlemozel* for so long, Puttbutt has a revelation and opts out of the whole program just as the conspiracy fails. The students finally mobilize after years of passive acceptance of their teachers' constant head games, and things almost return to status quo ante. Puttbutt shuffles off to Buffalo, or maybe it's Hawaii, end of novel, end.

After dismissing Puttbutt's self-involved world of academic specialization, which is solely preoccupied with merchandizing and commodifying the theoretical myopia of the moment, Reed added an Afterword, a personal epiphany on multicultural America he experienced on a spring day in Oakland, California, at a large ethnic festival of food and dance. Outside the Ivory Tower lived the authentic unmediated ethnicity of the "real" people, and here he poetically and succinctly provided the perspective the novel lacked. With this premeditated though unexpected act of literary and creative sabotage, Reed implied that the old civilities and literary conventions that formerly governed the academic world have broken down, and the postmodern forms* that are supposed to replace them are incoherent and divisive, with contradictory and criminal consequences for those involved within and without the academy.

Again what makes *Japanese by Spring* so entertaining is that like most of his other novels, Reed's satiric vision informs as well as entertains the reader. Sprinkled throughout this narrative (and essential too!) are barbed and explicit observations on Japanese culture and language and American Far Eastern foreign policy, as well as the linguistic and philosophic quirks of Yoruba language and culture (he is talking about African-American cultural studies after all). Much like *Mumbo Jumbo*, this novel is also an instamatic of contemporary multicultural American experience. However, this richly intriguing tapestry is contrasted and filtered through the tunnel vision of contemporary academia where Puttbutt plies his trade. It is a world of status-obsessed intellectuals engaged in ideological turf wars to promote their ascendence to the pinnacle of the ever-changing Theoretical Top 100 List, a world where the satisfaction of mentoring students is small beer compared to the rush of instant celebrity that comes with being a Theory Expert, a featured and well-remunerated speaker at academic conferences, someone with *serious grown-up power* capable of commanding large

199

---

*There is no point getting into an argument about what "postmodernism" really means, because half the fun of the term is writing about it, and writing, and writing. It's like some kind of universal decontextualized widget. It could be alternatively called the "present present," which is modified by variable contemporary media, or even "the corruptible future present," but it's still just another convenient nonspecific packaging metaphor trying to supplant terms like The Jazz Age, The Aspirin Age, The Silent Generation, The Beat Generation, The Blank Generation, and of course The X-Generation, a generic adjectival phrase that categorizes ideas, trends, and attitudes that haven't come into being yet. Postmodernism is probably one of the more egregious and newest of "weasel words" coined by academe yet. It certainly provides work for a lot of people (I wish it kept them thinking) and encourages them to fistfight at conferences and in the pages of journals, doesn't it?

study grants or corporate sponsorship for an *institute* as a well as an agent to book celebrity appearances.

It is a world where everyone is fighting everyone else for a piece of the ideological pie and its attendant spoils. In Puttbutt's case, that means in his immediate universe everyone from the high-fiving, jive-talking, dashiki-wearing head of African studies who's afraid he's losing his touch with the younger "bros" in the 'hood to his owlish English department counterpart, who's worried whether his PC quotient is sufficient to deal with the feminists who control the gender and women's studies subdivision and who themselves are intent on deconstructing the English department from inside out to promote their unique but equally myopic vision of American cultural life. This is a creepy world of ideological coups and countercoups that makes the Stalinist purge trials of the late thirties a comparative pink tea. Quite obviously, it's not a happy place to work and it's begging for a strong hand to put it out of its misery and start over, exactly what the conspirators have in mind.

It's easy to dismiss *Japanese by Spring* as just another academic novel, since writers have been using higher education as a fictional backdrop for years (those who work within and without it, from Kingsley Amis's *Lucky Jim* to Richard Farina's *Been Down So Long It Looks Like Up To Me* to David Lodge's *Changing Places* and *Small World* to most recently Robert Grudin's *Book*). It's a great format to use to get it all off one's chest, to indulge in some merciless lampooning of one's enemies, to right wrongs, to settle old scores, and, in the process, to endow one's allies (friends and lovers) with godlike qualities. If it's cleverly done, there's no foul, no fault, and nothing changes really.

If the satire is too transparent, you're in trouble and you be gone. At the worst this means being exiled to some kind of academic Siberia after being publicly drummed out of the fellowship, your writing slate broken and your academic gown rent by your departmental chair during an open faculty senate meeting. Barring that you may find a horse head in your bed one evening with a courtesy card from the Faculty Club.

On the other hand, if you're well-known and ornery enough, you'll be the new kick-me icon, target practice for sniping "think" pieces in mainstream literary magazines, Sunday morning TV talk shows, or ivory tower interdisciplinary institutional journals.

Ishmael Reed *has* tenure and *is* ornery by nature; his metaphorical back, like Moby Dick's, is mottled by an intricate network of overgrown scar tissue composed of broken-off harpoons, the detritus from all the hits he's taken for his outspokenness over the years. His is no ordinary academic novel by any stretch of the imagination, since for the Ish, these are not normal times. In attempting to cast the academy wars in a satiric light, he winds up demolishing the whole convention by inserting himself into his own book, though by trashing his work, he succeeds in bringing to the reader a more immediate sense of the desperation he feels at the current situation on American college campuses.

201

Instead of providing and encouraging an intellectual climate in which debates about meanings are welcomed, where open-ended conclusions are arrived at, in Puttbutt's world, and by extension in the world of higher education in general, debates center around the meaning of meanings, or better, the meaning of the *appearance* of meanings, though both are in reality nothing more than a marketeers' quest for designer packaging (or repackaging, as is so often the case). These days there is only information to be gleaned, insight is transitory and peripheral, an add-on. It's more the stuff of the smoke and mirrors, this business of consumer advertising for market dominance, and less a case of even-handed scholarship than the emphasis on the "cutting-edge" celebrity endorsement that confers a spurious authority.

If we follow Reed's view further, in this "hot" media world it just won't do for a teacher of undergraduates to say that there are no definitive answers to philosophical or ethical problems, only questions and approaches, despite the fact that society at large is predisposed to the belief and expectation that not only does everything have quantifiable answers, but there are invariant "right" ones to which exact formulas can be applied as an alchemical solvent. It's questionable science, if indeed that's the point, and even worse pedagogy. It's also a rude awakening for young minds who have been previously indoctrinated otherwise in primary and secondary school to be told by those from whom they hope to become credentialed that education broadens the periphery of one's ignorance, and accordingly that learning is a lifelong process, where a B.A. opens the door instead of closing it. Anyway, that's not what their parents or they themselves are paying for, is it? Practical useful knowledge for the money—right?

Higher education should be a dangerous and heady drug, a liberating experience though not when reduced to the marketplace where ideas themselves become nothing more than staged events, set pieces that the performer uses for entertainment.[5] If the pursuit of knowledge is nothing more than an exercise in professorial performance art, then it reinforces in students' minds that ideas have no validity outside of their immediate utility as entertainment, and thus in the same way one comparison shops for cars, one can comparison shop for ideas, from which follows the assumption that like any other consumer good, one can "trade up" or "retool" the engine of ideology. Higher education in this light is nothing more than a slightly advanced version of the high school life adjustment curriculum that has been an intellectual tonic in public secondary school education since the fifties, whose basis, as intellectual historian Richard Hofstader observed, is

> the more immediately usable an item of knowledge is, the more readily it can be taught. The value of a school subject can be

measured by the number of immediate, actual life situations to which it directly applies. The important thing, then, is not to teach pupils how to generalize, but to supply them directly with the information they need for daily living—for example, to teach them, not physiology, but how to keep physically fit.[4]

If we take Reed's satirical riffs "to the bridge," so to speak, he's pointing out that to carry over this view to higher education for whatever misguided motives is criminal and intellectually dishonest, because it ignores the profound long-term consequences not only for the undergraduates who eventually leave the academy, but also for the teachers (who should know better) who, by giving in, have broken faith with their craft and disregarded what they know in their hearts to be true. By promoting their own fashionable orthodoxies, they have reduced scholarship to an arena of competing products arrayed in the upscale mall of higher education. In doing so, they consciously reinforce the idea that higher learning requires nothing more than the comparison shopper's ability to make the "right" choices from the "right" answers that are already conveniently premixed and predigested for them. If this line of reasoning is carried to its logical conclusion, colleges and universities will be nothing more than purveyors of consumer guides whose diplomas eventually will be imprinted with expiration dates on the backs of the sheepskins—nice and convenient, but no cigar. Why?

This intellectual *fait accompli* encourages students to be lazy, spoiled, and intolerant, while promoting a lifelong cynicism for any kind of intellectual activity save for that which can be digested in a 20-second MTV buzz clip. Though students somehow survive and even thrive in this system, the end result robs them of their powers of discernment as well as their ability to think and reason on their own. They are cut loose, set adrift at sea with a defective compass that knows no true north. In short, academics are being honorable neither to their higher calling nor to their students, and honor is the glue that cements the compact between professors and students. It does not lie in rhetorical posturings, facile ratiocinations, or ideological marriages of convenience that ignore long-term consequences. Maybe it's not the loss of honor after all, but rather a lack of brass balls, since it takes incredible courage to tilt against an official educational ideology as well as a culture in which students are rewarded, encouraged to be, in the words of Benjamin J. Barber, "society smart rather than school smart . . . [where] their teachers in that world, the nation's true pedagogues, are television, advertising, movies, politics, and the celebrity domains they define."[5]

It's a tough audience to please, this postmodern student bunch who are comparison-shopping for cutting-edge informercials, for zappy bon mots to download to their disks. Maybe this is progress after all, and it's a good thing that academics have found a method for enlivening their formerly fusty profession by expropriating the trappings of the hot media world of art. It may appear to be a much sexier universe with more perks, better girls (boys), and money than working as an intellectual, a solitary thinker/teacher; it's the American dream perhaps having it all, but they've only got it half right. Blinded by the klieg lights of momentary media celebrity, they miss the downside that is the killer.

It is a profoundly antiintellectual world in which they ply the trade of thinking within a society predicated on a decontextualized present; it requires courage to go against the grain, to encourage reflection and the importance of living in the present informed by the presence of the past. It takes a foolhardy kind of chutzpa once the rules of the road have been lodged, but anything less is unacceptable if academics really want to assume their duties as serious intellectuals. If academics wish to portray themselves as performance artists, then they must also accept the transient politics of the art world that thrives on commodification and celebrity as well as its dangers like other savvy pragmatist "artists" whose lifestyles they wish to expropriate. According to Richard Schickel in *Intimate Strangers: The Culture of Celebrity,* he (or she) falls into celebrity trap via the publicizing process

> [which] gives him a status in the society that he might not have found in other eras, a sort of demi-heroism, [which] at the same time denies him that later heroism that a life self-sacrificingly devoted to his calling formerly conferred, especially on creators who were understood to be ahead in their time—a posterity of truly heroic proportions, which proportions can only be shaped out of mystery.[6]

When mainlined into the academic world, this publicity process devalues whatever knowledge teachers have a handle on and is, in effect, a conscious repudiation of the ideals they had before the theory dance started a decade or so ago, when the pickings and perks were leaner, when being an intellectual meant something to people like Vaclev Havel, who, to borrow a cliché from another sexy media world, the music business, had to "suffer to play the blues," and who courageously accepted that suffering as the price one pays for getting out of, in the words of Bob Dylan in yet another context, "going through all these things twice." Maybe it's simply a matter of consumer satisfaction that there's no longer any kick in being a guide and mentor. Possibly it's just an old-fashioned intellectual elitist conceit that has been replaced by something more au courant, newer, and deadlier, a marketplace elitism, as Richard Schickel notes "in which all success is measured quantitatively rather than qualitatively and critically."[7] Ars longa, pecunia longer? Who's to choose and who's to lose?

205

On a more basic level, though, this is a death wish of gigantic and tragic proportions, a bad game where everyone collegially lies to feel better while everyone loses big time: professors, students, and society. There is nothing sadder and more pathetic than being a victim of fashion. It may be the stuff of future talk shows from pop culture pundits or psychologists who service the sartorially and culturally challenged in the upper echelons of California, New York, or Chicago; surely the Internet bulletin board will be abuzz in some backwater roadhouse on the information superhighway eventually or even now. Be that as it may, it's still criminal to support a system that makes the difficult and frustrating search for knowledge irrelevant. If higher education is to serve higher ends instead of merely being a white collar credentialing mill in the postindustrial age, then college professors need to resubscribe and/or renew their faith in the Havel doctrine or else they wind up taking the heat from Abdul's progeny and become casualties themselves when some new game package or flashier huckster comes along to displace them. It may mean getting lower collective marks on student evaluation sheets for demanding quality work, but it's a risk that must be assumed.

206

Lest anyone think these kinds of arguments or observations are of our current coinage at the end of this century, one could do no better than to refer to those of educator, social scientist, and founder of Clark University, G. Stanley Hall (see Chapter 5, "Play School"). Gainsayers will protest no doubt that Hall's observations are invalid because he was writing about adolescence at the end of the nineteenth century, before electronic mass media changed everything and everybody, or because he was a friend and colleague of William James, he "shrouded the social problems of adolescence in the pseudoscientific jargons of psychology and biology"[8] (and so much for James too!). They will roll their eyes and point out Hall was also a contemporary of progressive educator and thinker John Dewey, who's an official nonperson now save on ceremonial occasions or, I suspect, and more to the point, that Granville Stanley Hall was just plain elitist and as everyone knows, elitism is not PC in these final decades of the Century of the Common Man. Hall's adolescents may or may not have worn knickers and parted their hair down the middle or been media-challenged, but even back then, good college teachers still knew what they had to do to ignite the spark of adolescent intellectual curiosity—as the good ones do today.

Hall wrote from a kinder, gentler sense of academic time and perspective, less publicity- and celebrity-ridden, true, but nevertheless his thoughts have direct resonance today for those who embrace the idea that with each new generation of undergraduates there is new hope for society, and it is the duty of the college teacher to act as its midwife. It is to speak to this spirit of intellectual renewal and evolution that college teaching aspires and that does not lie in the promulgation of transient fashions or in being intoxicated by the drug of momentary celebrity. When one says aloud to a group of questing minds, "I don't know, but let's see how we can find it out," instead of "It's in the book (or video)," that love of learning and inquiry is passed on. In the present tense atmosphere of huckstering and posturing, it's refreshing to find someone like Hall who laid it on the line even if a century ago:

> If professors made it always a point of honor to confess and never conceal the limitation of their knowledge, would scorn all pretense of it, place credit for originality frankly where it belongs, teach no creeds they do not profoundly believe, or topics in which they are not interested, and withhold nothing from those who want the truth, they could from this vantage with more effect bring students to feel that the laziness [the characteristic student apathy toward "doing the reading before the lecture" many professors meet on a daily basis], that while outwardly conforming does no real inner work, that getting a diploma, as a professor lately said, an average student could do on one hour's study a day, living beyond one's means, and thus imposing a hardship on parents greater than the talent of the sons justifies, accepting stipends not needed, especially to the deprivation of those more needy, using dishonest ways of securing rank in studies or positions, on teams, or social standing, are one and all, not only ungentlemanly but cowardly and mean, and the axe would be laid at the root of the tree.[9]

Hall wasn't the only lumberjack wielding the axe out there in the groves of American academe 100 years ago. He joined William James, a distinguished polymath, psychologist, and humanist, who'd done so earlier in an essay written for the Harvard Monthly in 1903. In "The Ph.D. Octopus," James observed from inside the Harvard academic establishment that the degree itself not only conferred an inappropriate and overblown reputation for erudition and scholarship within the academy but outside it was "in point of fact already looked upon as a mere advertising resource, a manner of throwing dust in the Public's eye."[10] It was, moreover, playing into the disturbing trend Americans already had to revere titles,[11] which sounds familiar enough to us when confronted with the variety of Ph.D. programs in everything from physical therapy to real estate management today.

Of course he was referring to an earlier, more innocent academic age when in American colleges and universities there was a dearth of homegrown scholars, where the prestige doctorates still came from the great old universities in Germany. Back in those dear dead days, the Ph.D. was distinguished by its scarcity, the M.A., less so, and teaching and scholarship proceeded for the most part without anything other than perhaps a B.A. It was innocently thought back then in that characteristic American quantifiable way that the more Ph.D.'s one had on the faculty, the better the school. Then as now there were individuals who did the dance gracefully and easily, who "pass with ease all ordeals with which life confronts them,"[12] and those who succeeded by dint of intestinal fortitude and a thick skin though "not without baleful nervous wear and tear and retardation of their purely inner life, but on the whole successfully, and with advantage."[13]

The octopus's main victims were all the other candidates, in fact the great majority for whom (as can be seen in any number of academic novels over the years, including Reed's persona-damaged one) the doctoral degree dance was (and is) a humiliating intellectual experience. For the journeyman scholar "without marked originality or native force, but fond of truth and especially of books and study, ambitious of reward and recognition, poor often, and needing a degree to get a teaching position, weak in the eyes of their examiners,"[14] it was a poisonous hell that one survived damaged and temporarily enervated of intellectual curiosity in the short term. Ironically, in the longer term, once over the immediate effects, these same recovering damaged scholars tended to perpetuate unconsciously the humiliations they underwent on future candidates—a little bondage, a little humiliation in the exercise of dominance, just like a fraternity hazing.

For James, not only was this state of affairs insupportably dishonest and outrageous, but it also undercut the tenets of scholarship and free inquiry he had always championed throughout his long and productive life:

> To interfere with the free development of talent, to obstruct the natural play of supply and demand in the teaching profession, to foster academic snobbery by the prestige of certain privileged institutions, to transfer accredited value from essential manhood to an outward badge, to blight hopes and promote invidious sentiments, to divert the attention of aspiring youth from direct dealings with truth to the passing of examinations—such consequences, if they exist, ought surely to be regarded as drawbacks to the system, and an enlightened public consciousness ought to be keenly alive to the importance of reducing their amount.[15]

Not! Unfortunately, these are the signature characteristics and perverse "strengths" of the contemporary American academic experience that *Japanese by Spring* satirically explored before Reed lost his patience and his cool. Despite his failure or maybe because of it, Reed put his finger upon the weaknesses that have been bedeviling higher education for more than 100 years. Can you blame him if he could find no satiric resolution and bailed out in disgust?

Though we may have commenced this essay innocently enough by examining a failed academic novel, we nevertheless wind up gaping open-mouthed at the spectacle of Camille Paglia in black leather and holding a whip, renegade feminist, anarchic Shiva, and academic black sheep bad girl, being profiled in *People* and *Time* magazines for her theories on litera-

ture, life, sex, and death. It's the very image that the Ish may
have been pointing toward, one supposes, the logical end result:
the *dominatrix academensis,* the souped-up nineties academic
version of Betty Page, fifties America's bondage pin-up, whose
iconography itself echoed back to earlier Victorian days of Hall
and James. In a strange way, though, that's one hell of a vision
of the present informed by a presence of the past for you: What
starts with mumbo jumbo ends with black leather. And even if
the Ish failed to bring it off completely, he succeeded in piquing
our curiosity and exercising our insight, which is, after all, far
better than simply striking a pose and vogueing for the cameras,
don't you think?

Da Capo

Back to the head—and that's our *Teenage Nervous Breakdown*. So where do we go from here? The problem's way too big for me to deal with, Walley. Having read this book, you're entitled to ask that question, but unfortunately I can offer no definitive answers, nor did I intend to. For one thing, I wanted these essays to be descriptive rather than prescriptive. You have to know what the problem is and how it manifests itself before definitive action can be taken. Nonetheless, what *is* obvious to anyone who gives a good goddamn is that the powers that be, the ConGlomCos great and small who actually run this world through the electronic media, bank on that fact that *not* only will you *not* give a damn or that you will merely *like*, but ultimately that you will *prefer* how they view the subtotal of your life. That's what I tried to show—damn, I hope I'm not right.

But since you asked, for better or worse, here's what I think: Maybe it starts simply enough with talking back at the TV set when your kids are around and you see something that's just totally bogus and you explain to them why. Things will change when people willfully opt to be informed and question the values of the consumer world, when people prefer not to be anesticized by those values and the goods they seem to represent (and know the difference between the two states), because knowledge is power. I'd say that all of this requires a revolution in our thinking, but "revolution" is too overused a term these days, applying just as readily to dish-washing liquid or 24-hour lipstick as social upheaval. Putting the Evolution back into Revolution is more to my point, because evolution starts with individuals, not consumer affinity groups or target audiences. In its purest form as a cultural statement, that's what I thought the six-ties were all about. Evolution had to do with discovering a series of truths that had always been there waiting for me and my gen-eration to rediscover; naively we had hoped future generations would also uncover the same ones as part of their growth, too. That's what happens when one leaves high school behind for-ever. Boil that down to this: Each generation has a duty to in-form the next that the rules of the road have nothing to do with music TV or the consumer world it has birthed.

All of this may indeed be happening, and perhaps I'm not just seeing it yet, though I'm thinking that I should have by now. We can only do the best we can to live up to our potential, but it is crucially important that what is "the best" keeps being fur-ther refined and defined: That's what I was reaching for in this book.

Hope you enjoyed the set.

Notes

Preface

1. Vonnegut, Kurt, *Wampeters, Foma & Granfalloons* (New York: Delacorte, 1974).

1. "This, Here, Soon"

1. Huizinga, Johan, *America: A Dutch Historian's Vision, From Afar and Near,* translated by Herbert H. Rowen (New York: Harper & Row, 1972), p. 168.

2. Copyright Peggy Garrison 1972 and used with permission.

3. Ostrander, Gilbert, *American Civilization in the First Machine Age* (New York: Harper & Row, 1970), p. 224.

4. de Tocqueville, Alexis, *Democracy in America,* edited and abridged by Richard D. Heffner (New York: New American Library, 1964), p. 213.

5. Whitman, Walt, *Prose Works 1892–Volume II, Collected and Other Prose,* edited by Floyd Stoval (New York: NYU Press, 1964), pp. 402–403.

6. "Survey: Too Much Television, Fat in Children's Diet," Associated Press, September 20, 1994.

7. Whitman, p. 474.

8. Pound, Ezra, "Hugh Selwyn Mauberly" (first published in 1920), *Personal: Collected Poems of Ezra Pound* (New York: Horace Liveright, 1926).

9. Huizinga, p. 168.

10. Harountunian, Joseph, *Lust for Power* (New York: Charles Scribner's Sons, 1949), p. 19.

11. Bryson, Bill, *The Lost Continent: Travels in Small-Town America* (New York: Harper & Row, 1989), p. 130.

12. Walley, David G., *The Ernie Kovacs Phile* (New York: Fireside Books, 1987), p. 207.

13. Bloom, Allan, *The Closing of the American Mind: How Higher Education Has Failed Democracy and Impoverished the Souls of Today's Students* (New York: Simon & Schuster, 1987), p. 73.

14. Bloom, p. 75.

15. Walley, David, *No Commercial Potential: The Saga of Frank Zappa* (New York: Da Capo Press, 1996), p. 201.

16. Walley, p. 201.

2. Who Stole the Bomp (from the Bomp Sha Bomp)?

1. Frith, Simon, *Music for Pleasure: Essays in the Sociology of Pop* (New York: Routledge, 1988), p. 4.

2. Ward, Ed, "Dedicated to You" in *Stranded: Rock and Roll for a Desert Island,* edited by Greil Marcus (New York: Da Capo Press, 1996), pp. 248–249.

3. Torches, Nick, *Country: The Twisted Roots of Rock 'n' Roll* (New York: Da Capo Press, 1996).

4. For a more worked-out account of this mini culture war, see R. Serge Denisoff's *Tarnished Gold: The Record Industry Revisited* (New Brunswick, NJ: Transaction Books, 1986).

5. Willis, Ellen, "Velvet Underground: Golden Archive Series," *Stranded: Rock and Roll for a Desert Island,* edited by Greil Marcus (Da Capo Press: New York, 1996) p. 73.

6. It should be noted here that the amount of press generated is no guarantee of commercial success. CBS in the early seventies even went as far as announcing in the trades that a Blood, Sweat and Tears album had been shipped gold, i.e., had sold 100,000 units; unfortunately, it came *back* gold too—we all laughed.

7. Rockwell, John, "Living in the USA," in *Stranded: Rock and Roll for a Desert Island*, edited by Greil Marcus (New York, Da Capo Press, 1996), p. 188.

8. I should know. I was the boyfriend. For further details, see *Strange Days: My Life With and Without Jim Morrison* by Patricia Kennealy (New York: Dutton, 1992).

9. For a very impressive and exhaustive history of the punk movement in England, see John Savage, *England's Dreaming* (New York: St. Martin's Press, 1992).

10. NcNeil, Legs, and Gillian McCain, *Please Kill Me: The Uncensored Oral History of Punk* (New York: Grove Press, 1996), p. 299

11. McNeil and McCain, p. 334.

12. Ostrander, Gilbert, *American Civilization in the First Machine Age* (New York: Harper & Row, 1970), p. 20.

13. Ward, p. 151.

3. Blame It on the Sixties

1. Hugh F. Kenner and Don Gifford, correspondence, 1983.

2. Bloom, Allan, *The Closing of the American Mind: How Higher Education Has Failed Democracy and Impoverished the Souls of Today's Students* (New York: Simon & Schuster, 1987), p. 333.

3. Davis, Fred, *Yearning for Yesterday: A Sociology of Nostalgia* (New York: The Press, 1979), p. 31.

4. Davis, p. 111.

5. Davis, p. 122.

6. Geertz, Clifford, *Local Knowledge: Further Essays in Interpretative Anthropology* (New York: Basic Books, 1983), p. 44.

7. See Herbert Gans, *Deciding What's News* (New York: Pantheon Books, 1979), for an accurate assessment of how news is textured and "spun" for public consumption to meet the needs of advertising and ratings by major television news producers and editorial directors. Though his writing style is somewhat stilted, the information is invaluable.

8. Jones, Landon Y., *Great Expectations: America and the Baby Boom Generation* (New York: Coward, McCann and Geoghegen, 1980), p. 68. This well-written basic text lead me to Davis's valuable discussion on nostalgia as a driving force in commercial culture in general and in the sixties in particular. It should be read in conjunction with Abe Peck's *Uncovering the Sixties: The Life and Times of the Underground Press* (New York: Pantheon Books, 1985).

9. James, William, *The Varieties of Religious Experience* (New York: Modern Library Random House, 1902), p. 380n.

10. Clampitt, Amy, *The Kingfisher* (New York: Knopf, 1985), p. 57.

11. Whitman, Walt, *Prose Works 1892–Volume II* (New York: NYU Press, 1964), p. 370.

12. Whitman, p. 396.

13. For an in-the-trenches view of the complexities of cultural revolution sixties-style, one can do no better than read Abe Peck's *Uncovering the Sixties: The Life and Times of the Underground Press* (New York: Pantheon Books, 1985). He manages to give the era a precise, interconnected, and intelligently informed chronology that perfectly captures the spirit, intensity, contradictions, and triumphs. It's the next best thing to having been there. Having been there myself as an underground journalist at New York's *East Village Other* from 1969 to 1973, I happen to agree with him, so there will be some similarities in our approaches if not conclusions in my chapter analysis.

14. For a real example of the mind-set of the media politics and headgames that in some small part contributed to the chaos of the '68 Chicago Convention, see poet, musician, and critic Ed Sanders' *Shards of God: a Novel of the Yippies* (New York: Grove Press, 1970). It could be history, and maybe even is, from one of the era's more articulate and creative "spokesmen."

15. Walley, David, "Abbie in Noshville: The Miami Convention," 1972 (unpublished ms.).

16. Kett, Joseph, *Rites of Passage: Adolescence in America 1790–present* (New York: Basic Books, 1977) p. 272.

17. Kip Cohen, interview by the author, December 20, 1970.

18. Leach, William, *Land of Desire: Merchants, Power and the Rise of a New American Culture* (New York: Pantheon Books, 1993), p. 37.

19. Kennealy, Patricia. "Woodstock '69." in *Jazz and Pop Magazine*, vol. 8, no. 11 (November 1969), p. 22.

20. For a sympathetic account of the Altamont Concert and its aftermath, see *Altamont: Death of Innocence in the Woodstock Nation*, edited and introduction by Jonathon Eisen (New York: Avon, 1970). See specifically "Paradise Loused" by Andy Gordon for a cinematic Mailer-esque account of the concert and the cultural mind-set surrounding it.

21. Cohen, interview by author.

22. Cohen, interview by author.

23. Huizinga, J.H., *In the Shadow of History* (New York: W.W. Norton, 1936). p. 178.

4. Boxers or Briefs?

1. Walley, David. *Decadent Memories* (unpublished manuscript, 1980).

2. Pielke, Robert G., *You Say You Want a Revolution: Rock Music in American Culture* (Chicago: Nelson-Hall, 1986), p. 18.

3. Walley, David, *No Commercial Potential: The Saga of Frank Zappa* (New York: Da Capo Press, 1996), p. 203.

4. This paragraph and the one below have been adapted from Walley, *No Commercial Potential*.

5. "Wal-Mart's CD Standards Are Changing Pop Music." *New York Times* (November 12, 1996), pp. 1, 12.

5. Play School

1. Huizinga, Johan. *Homo Ludens.* (London: Routledge & Kegan Paul Ltd., 1949), p. 193.

2. Hall, G. Stanley, *Adolescence: Its Psychology and Its Relation to Physiology. Anthropology, Sociology, Sex, Crime, Religion and Education, Volumes I & II* (New York: D. Appleton and Company, 1907), Volume I, p. xv.

3. Hall, Volume I, pp. xvi–xvii ff.

4. Hall, Volume II, p. 411.

5. Hall, Volume II, p. 488.

6. Hall, Volume II, p. 362.

7. Hall, Volume II, p. 496.

8. Hofstader, Richard, *Anti-Intellectualism in America* (New York: Knopf, 1963), p. 237.

9. Hofstader, p. 342.

10. Hofstader, p. 350.

11. Hofstader, p. 356.

12. See the study by the National Education Commission on Time and Learning cited in Catherine Manegold's "Only 41% of U.S. Schools Day Spent on Academic Subjects," *New York Times* (May 5, 1994), p. 1.

13. Edward Zwick, a creator of *Thirtysomething,* quoted in Bernard Weintraub's "In Hollywood, a Party Is a Party, and an Awards Show Is Even Better," *New York Times,* (January 23, 1994), p. C11.

14. Ostrander, Gilbert, *American Civilization in the First Machine Age* (New York: Harper & Row, 1970), p. 20.

15. Friedenberg, Edgar Z., *The Vanishing Adolescent* (Boston: Beacon Press, 1959, 1964), p. 8.

16. Eckert, Penelope, *Jocks and Burnouts: Social Categories and Identity in the High School* (New York: Teachers College Press, 1989), p. 12.

17. Brake, Michael, *Comparative Youth Culture,* (Boston: Routledge & Kegan Paul, 1985), p. 16.

18. Friedenberg, p. 11.

6. The Twinkie Defense

1. Schickel, Richard, *Intimate Strangers: The Culture of Celebrity* (New York: Doubleday & Co., 1985), p. 289.

2. Schickel, p. 289.

3. de Tocqueville, Alexis, *Democracy in America* (New York: Washington Square Press, 1965). See especially Chapter 35, "Peculiar Effects of the Love of Physical Gratification in Democratic Times."

7. Asking Alice

1. "Fab Four's Album Sales Soar," *The Transcript*, North Adams, MA, Associated Press, October 22, 1996, p. 16.

2. Latimer, Dean, and Jeff Goldberg; *Flowers in the Blood: The Story of Opium* (New York: Franklin Watts, 1981), p. 180.

3. Latimer and Goldberg, p. 190.

4. Latimer and Goldberg, p. 190.

5. Latimer and Goldberg, p. 190.

6. Latimer and Goldberg, footnote, pp. 227–228.

7. Kenner, Hugh F., *A Sinking Island, "Bards and Bard-Watchers,"* (New York: Knopf, 1988), p. 254.

8. Don't Touch Me There

1. de Tocqueville, Alexis; *Democracy in America* (New York: Washington Square Press, 1965). See Chapter 35: Peculiar Effects of "The Love of Physical Gratification in Democratic Times."

2. Newman, Eric, *The Great Mother* (Princeton, NJ: Princeton University Press, 1955), p. 35.

9. White Punks on Dope

1. Havel, Vaclav, *Disturbing the Peace* (New York: Knopf, 1990), p. 167.

2. Reed, Ishmael, *Mumbo Jumbo* (New York: Bantam Books, 1973), p. 42.

3. Schickel, Richard, *Intimate Strangers: The Culture of Celebrity* (New York: Doubleday & Co., 1985), p. 139.

4. Hofstader, Richard, *Anti-Intellectualism in America* (New York: Knopf, 1963), p. 346.

5. Barber, Benjamin J., "America Skips School," *Harper's Magazine* (December 1993), p. 40. This is an excerpt adapted from Barber's book *An Aristocracy for Everyone: The Politics of Education and the Future of America* (New York: Ballantine Books, 1992). It's a passionate piece of scholarship that centers on the argument that schools ought to provide training in citizenship. His discussion of political correctness, Alan Bloom's *Closing of the American Mind* controversy, is well-written, witty, concise, and a good primer for those who follow this bubbling tempest— and he's far more polite than Reed when he takes on the canon.

6. Schickel, p. 223.

7. Schickel, p. 242.

8. Nasaw, David, *Schooled to Order: A Social History of Public Schooling in the United States* (New York: Oxford University Press, 1979), p. 88.

9. Hall, G. Stanley, *Adolescence, Vol. II* (New York: D. Appleton and Company, 1907), pp. 400 ff.

10. James, William, *William James: Writings 1902–1910* (New York: The Library of America, 1987), pp. 1112 ff.

11. "It is indeed odd to see this love of titles—and such titles—growing up in a country of which the recognition of individuality and bare manhood have so long been supposed to be the very soul" (James, p. 1118).

12. James, p. 1115.

13. James.

14. James, pp. 1115 ff.

15. James, p. 1114.

Selected Bibliography

Aronowitz, Stanley, *Roll Over Beethoven: The Return of Cultural Strife* (Middletown, CT: Wesleyan University Press, 1993).

Barber, Benjamin J., *An Aristocracy for Everyone: The Politics of Education and the Future of America* (New York: Ballantine Books, 1992).

Bell, Bernard Iddings, *Crisis in Education* (New York: Whittlesey House, 1949).

Bledstein, Burton, *The Culture of Professionalism: The Middle Class and the Development of Higher Education in America* (New York: Norton, 1976).

Bloom, Allan, *The Closing of the American Mind: How Higher Education Has Failed Democracy and Impoverished the Souls of Today's Students* (New York: Simon & Schuster, 1987).

Boorstin, Daniel J., *The Americans: The Democratic Experience* (New York: Random House, 1973).

Boorstin, Daniel J., *The Image: A Guide to Pseudo-Events in America* (New York: Athenaeum, 1980) (originally *The Image: What Happened to the American Dream*, New York: Athenaeum, 1961).

Brake, Michael, *Comparative Youth Culture* (Boston: Routledge & Kegan Paul, 1985).

Braudel, Fernand, *On History*, translated by Sarah Matthews (Chicago: University of Chicago Press, 1980).

Bryson, Bill, *The Lost Continent: Travels in Small-Town America* (New York: Harper & Row, 1989).

Caillois, Roger, *Man, Play, and Games,* translated by Meyer Barash (London, UK: Thames and Hudson, 1962).

Buzzi, Giancarlo, *Advertising: Its Cultural and Political Effects* (Minneapolis: University of Minnesota Press, 1968).

Coleman, James S., *The Adolescent Society: The Social Life of the Teenager and Its Impact on Education* (Glencoe, IL: Free Press, 1962).

Cremer, Lawrence, *The Transformation of the School: Progressivism in American Education 1876–1957* (New York, 1961).

Dallek, Robert, *The American Style of Foreign Policy: Cultural Politics and Foreign Affairs* (New York: Knopf, 1983).

Davis, Fred, *Yearning for Yesterday: A Sociology of Nostalgia* (New York: Free Press, 1979).

Denisoff, R. Serge, *Tarnished Gold: The Record Industry Revisited* (New Brunswick, NJ: Transaction Books, 1986).

Donavel, David F., *High School: The American Walkabout* (Andover, MA: The Regional Laboratory, 1995).

Dragastin, Sigmund, and Glen Elder, editors, *Adolescence and the Life Cycle* (New York: Wiley, 1975).

Eckert, Penelope, *Jocks and Burnouts: Social Categories and Identity in the High School* (New York: Teachers College Press, 1989).

Ehrenfeld, David, *Beginning Again* (New York: Oxford University Press, 1993).

Ehrenreich, Barbara, *The Hearts of Men* (New York: Anchor Books, 1984).

Eliot, Marc, *Rockenomics: The Money Behind the Music* (New York: Franklin Watts, 1989).

Fass, Paula S. *The Damned and the Beautiful: American Youth in the 1920s* (New York: Oxford University Press, 1977).

Feuer, Louis, *The Conflict of Generations* (New York: Basic Books, 1969).

Foley, Douglas, *Learning Capitalist Culture: Deep in the Heart of Texas* (Philadelphia: University of Pennsylvania Press, 1990).

Friedenberg, Edgar Z., *The Vanishing Adolescent* (Boston: Beacon Press, 1959, 1964).

Frith, Simon, *Music for Pleasure: Essays in the Sociology of Pop* (New York: Routledge, 1988).

Fritt, Simon, *Sound Effects: Youth, Leisure and the Politics of Rock 'n' Roll* (New York: Pantheon Books, 1981).

Fukuyama, Francis, *The End of History and the Last Man* (New York: Free Press, 1992).

225

Fuller, Robert C., *Americans and the Unconscious* (New York: Oxford University Press, 1986).

Gaines, Donna, *Teenage Wasteland* (New York: HarperCollins, 1990, 1991).

Garofolo, Reebee, editor, *Rockin' the Boat: Mass Music and Mass Movements* (Boston: South End Press, 1992).

Gillis, John, *Youth and History: Tradition and Change in European Age Relations, 1770–Present* (New York: Academic Press, 1981).

Goldman, E. F. *Two-Way Street* (Boston: Bellman Publishing Company, 1948).

Hall, G. Stanley, *Adolescence: Its Psychology and Its Relation to Physiology, Anthropology, Sociology, Sex, Crime, Religion and Education, Volumes I & II* (New York: D. Appleton and Company, 1907).

Harountunian, Joseph, *Lust for Power* (New York: Scribner, 1949).

Henry, Tricia, *Break All Rules! Punk Rock and the Making of a Style* (Ann Arbor, MI: UMI Research Press, 1989).

Hiner, N. Ray, and Joseph M. Hawed, editors, *American Childhood: A Research Guide and Historical Handbook* (Westport, CT: Greenwood Press, 1985).

Hofstader, Richard, *Anti-Intellectualism in America* (New York: Knopf, 1963).

Howe, Neil, and Bill Strauss, *13th Gen (Abort, Retry, Ignore, Fail?)* (New York: Vintage Books, 1993).

Huizinga, Johan, *America: A Dutch Historian's Vision, From Afar and Near,* translated by Herbert H. Rowen (Harper & Row: New York, 1972).

Huizinga, Johan, *Homo Ludens* (London: Routledge & Kegan Paul Ltd., 1949).

Huizinga, Johan, *In the Shadow of History* (New York: Norton, 1936).

James, William, *The Varieties of Religious Experience* (New York: Random House, 1902).

James, William, "The Ph.D. Octopus," in *The Harvard Monthly* (March 1903), from *William James: Writings 1902–1910* (New York: The Library of America, 1987).

Jezer, Marty, *The Dark Ages: Life in the United States, 1945–* (Boston: South End Press, 1982).

Jones, Landon Y., *Great Expectations: America and the Baby Boom Generation* (New York: Coward, McCann and Geoghegan, 1980).

Kett, Joseph F., *The Pursuit of Knowledge under Difficulties: From Self-Improvement to Adult Education in America, 1750–1990* (Stanford, CA: Stanford University Press, 1994).

Kett, Joseph F., *Rites of Passage: Adolescence in America 1790–present* (New York: Basic Books, 1977).

Kline, Stephen, *Out of the Garden: Toys and Children's Culture in the Age of TV Marketing* (New York: Verso, 1993).

Krug, Edward A., *The Shaping of the American High School 1920–1940* (Madison: University of Wisconsin Press, 1972).

Lanza, Joseph, *Elevator Music: A Surreal History of Muzak, Easy-Listening, and Other Moodsong* (New York: St. Martin's Press, 1994).

LaPiere, Richard, *The Freudian Ethic* (New York: Duell, Sloan and Pearce, 1959).

Lasch, Christopher, *The Culture of Narcissism: American Life in An Age of Diminishing Expectations* (New York: Norton, 1979).

Laswell, Harold D., *Democracy through Public Opinion* (New York: 1941).

Leach, William, *Land of Desire: Merchants, Power and the Rise of a New American Culture* (New York: Pantheon Books, 1993).

Lears, T. J. Jackson, *Fables of Abundance: A Cultural History of Advertising in America* (New York: Basic Books, 1994).

Livingston, James, *Pragmatism and the Political Economy of Cultural Revolution* (Chapel Hill, NC: UNC Press, 1994).

Lurie, Alison, *The Language of Clothes* (New York: Randon House, 1981).

Marcus, Greil, editor, *Stranded: Rock and Roll for a Desert Island* (New York: Da Capo Press, 1996).

Mathison, Richard R., *Faiths, Cults and Sects of America: From Atheism to Zen* (New York: Bobbs Merrill, 1960).

Meyer, Donald, *The Positive Thinkers: Popular Religious Psychology from Mary Baker Eddy to Norman Vincent Peale and Ronald Reagan* (Middletown, CT: Wesleyan University Press, 1988).

McNeil, Legs, and Gillian McCain, *Please Kill Me: The Uncensored Oral History of Punk* (New York: Grove Press, 1996).

Modell, John, *Into One's Own: From Youth to Adulthood in the United States 1920–1975* (Berkeley: University of California Press, 1989).

Nasaw, David, *Going Out: The Rise and Fall of Public Amusements* (New York: Basic Books, 1993).

Nasaw, David, *Schooled to Order: A Social History of Public Schooling in the United States* (New York: Oxford University Press), 1979.

Nock, Albert J., *The Memories of a Superfluous Man* (Chicago: Henry Regnery Company, 1942, 1964).

Nock, Albert J., *The Theory of Education in The United States* (New York: Harcourt, Brace and Company, 1932).

Orman, John, *The Politics of Rock Music* (Chicago: Nelson-Hall, 1994).

Ostrander, Gilbert, *American Civilization in the First Machine Age* (New York: Harper & Row, 1970).

Pattison, Robert, *The Triumph of Vulgarity: Rock Music in the Mirror of Romanticism* (New York: Oxford University Press, 1987).

Pielke, Robert G., *You Say You Want a Revolution: Rock Music in American Culture* (Chicago: Nelson-Hall, 1986).

Pollock, Bruce, *Hipper Than Our Kids: A Rock and Roll Journal of the Baby Boom Generation* (New York: Schirmer Books, 1993).

Rosenberg, Bernard, and David Manning White, *Mass Culture: The Popular Arts in America* (Glencoe, IL: Free Press, 1957).

Rossitor, Clinton, *Parties and Politics in America* (Ithaca, NY: Cornell University Press, 1960).

Roszak, Theodore. *The Making of a Counter Culture: Reflections on the Technocratic Society and Its Youthful Opposition* (New York: Doubleday, 1969).

Santayana, George. *Character and Opinion in the United States* (New York: Scribner's, 1920).

Scheurer, Timothy E., *Born in the U.S.A.: The Myth of America in Popular Music from Colonial Times to the Present* (Jackson: University of Mississippi Press, 1991).

Schickel, Richard. *Intimate Strangers: The Culture of Celebrity* (New York: Doubleday, 1985).

Scott, John, *Rebel Rock: The Politics of Popular Music* (Oxford, UK: Basil Blackwell, 1986).

Spring, Joel, *The Sorting Machine: National Education Policy since 1945* (New York: David McKay, 1976).

Strauss, Samuel. *American Opportunity* (Boston: Little, Brown, 1935).

Stuessy, Joe, *Rock and Roll: Its History and Stylistic Development* (Englewood Cliffs, NJ: Prentice-Hall, 1990).

Susman, Warren I., *Culture as History: The Transformation of American Society in the 20th Century* (New York: Pantheon Books, 1984).

Taylor, William R. editor, *Inventing Times Square: Commerce and Culture at the Crossroads of the World* (New York: Russell Sage Foundation, 1991).

de Tocqueville, Alexis, *Democracy in America* (New York: Washington Square Press, 1965).

Veblen, Thorstein, *The Theory of the Leisure Class: An Economic Study of Institutions* (New York: Random House, 1934).

Weinstein, Deena, *Heavy Metal: A Cultural Sociology* (New York: Lexington Books, 1991).

Whitman, Walt, *Prose Works 1892–Volume II, Collect and Other Prose,* edited by Floyd Stoval (New York: NYU Press, 1964).

Wicke, Peter, *Rock Music: Culture, Aesthetics and Sociology,* translated by Rachel Fogg, (London: Cambridge University Press, 1990).

Wilson, Edmund, *The Cold War and the Income Tax* (New York: Farrar Strauss, 1963).

Wood, Robert C. *Suburbia: Its People and Their Politics* (Boston: Houghton Mifflin, 1958).

Index